THE BEST OF CHILDREN'S
ART&
CRAFTS

The Australian Women's Weekly

about the book

The importance of art and craft projects for children cannot be overestimated. Creative play stimulates even the youngest child's imagination and, upon completion of the project, promotes a great sense of achievement.

This book features brilliant step-by-step projects that kids and adults will love. Where preparation is required, it is simple and fast and, if the project is particularly messy, we've included advice on cleaning up. The content is best suited to younger children, aged from two to eight. Older children may use their enthusiasm to take simple projects further, without the need for constant adult supervision.

The projects have been chosen to assist children in the growth of many skills, including concentration, small muscle development, hand-eye coordination, sensory discrimination, problem-solving and decision-making.

Ideal for parents, grandparents, teachers, play-group supervisors and those who train teachers, this book will provide all carers with good ideas and the means to carry them out. Kids will never be bored during school holidays again!

Most importantly, though, you should use this book to help develop your child's confidence and pride in his or her own ideas. If a child is inclined to copy what he or she sees in the photographs in this book, put the book out of sight. Encourage children to experiment – they need to know there is no one right way for their art to look when finished. Self-expression should be fun!

contents

guidelines &
equipment

Every preschool, kindergarten, community group or family where young children are involved in arts and crafts will need certain basic items. Look for supplies at variety and discount shops. However, when quality and safety are important, as with scissors, buy items in shops specialising in these requirements. Don't overlook though, the endless variety of materials found in nature that can be used for art and craft projects.

Age: we have suggested a minimum age for most projects as a guide to projects that may prove too difficult for younger children. ALL AGES means from two years upwards but these projects still require supervision. The ages given are a guide only, as children differ in their ability to master certain steps. With close supervision, younger children may be able to manage more difficult projects, although their attention span may not last until the project is finished. We have used the word 'adult' to show where help will be needed for very young children, or where toxic products or sharp instruments are to be used, or where cooking or heating is required.

basic items

Adhesive tape: invest in a heavy tape dispenser which is easy for children to use.

Brushes: should be at least 1½ cm (⁵⁄₈in) wide and have long handles (over 15cm [6in]). Occasionally fine-pointed brushes are needed for a particular project. Brushes should be cleaned in cold water and soap after use, and stored in a can with their bristles up or wrapped in newspaper. Provide a brush for each paint colour; if the brush has a coloured handle, match it with the paint colour to encourage children to return the brush to the original paint bowl.

Coloured chalk: avoid hard, scratchy chalk. Soft, brightly coloured chalk is relatively inexpensive and available from art and craft supplies stores.

Crayons: should be at least 13mm (½in) in diameter for children under five to use.

Small thin crayons break easily and are difficult for little fingers to grip. Child-care experts suggest breaking the crayons to overcome the child's apprehension of breaking them. Remove some of the wrapper to encourage full use.

Fabric crayons: are available from art and craft supplies stores. Designs must be heat-sealed according to the manufacturer's instructions.

Felt-tipped pens: are available in many colours. Ensure the pens are non-toxic. Also look for thick felt pens which are easier for small hands to grip.

Foil: any type of foil such as aluminium foil or tin foil can be used.

Glitter: easiest to use in a coarse salt shaker. Put a sheet of newspaper under the project. Shake the excess glitter onto the newspaper. Lift each side so that the glitter falls to the fold in the newspaper. Put one end of the fold onto the edge of the open salt shaker and lift paper to allow glitter to fall into shaker.

Needles: can be used by children over five years but they should be blunt and have a large eye, such as a bodkin or darning needle. When threading a needle, the end of the string must be stiff so children can push it through the needle hole easily. This can be done by either wrapping a piece of sticky tape around the end of the string or by dunking the end in melted wax and leaving it to set. When weaving wool, adhesive tape can be wrapped around the end of the wool to stiffen it as an alternative to using a needle.

Newsprint paper: is cheap and comes in colours. It absorbs liquid more than other paper and tears more easily. Ideal for easel painting. Available from printers' supplies shops.

Oil pastels: smooth and vividly coloured, they give the effect of oily chalk.

Paint rollers: use rollers as an alternative to paintbrushes.

Papier-mâché: a technique where pulped paper soaked in **paper paste** is moulded into shapes, or where objects are covered with strips of paper dipped into paper paste and then left to dry.

Plaster bandage: these are gauze bandages impregnated with plaster and available from chemists. To use, just wet the bandage and place over a mould. They dry quickly and are great for making masks and sculpture.

Plasticine: available in many colours. It can sometimes be hard for little hands to manipulate, especially in cold weather.

Scissors: cheap scissors are a waste of money because soon they will not cut without tearing. Spend a little more money on small scissors with a blunt end. Left-handed scissors are available at art and craft supplies stores.

Staplers: use medium-sized staplers, about 10cm (4in) to 15cm (6in), because purse-sized staplers break easily and large staplers are too difficult for children to press down.

paste & glues

Clear craft glue: more expensive than **PVA glue** and not as strong, although it's faster drying. It is particularly helpful in holding fabrics and laces in place, but will seep through fabrics if applied too liberally. It is harmful if eaten or inhaled.

Commercial liquid starch: can be purchased already made up in many stores. It has an indefinite storage life.

Commercial paper paste: any sort will do but the most vivid colours are achieved with paper paste made for lightweight wallpapers, hobbies and crafts. Follow the directions using cold water and stir briskly while adding the powder and for a minute afterwards. It often has lumps at first, but these usually disappear in a few hours. Commercial paper paste has no fungicide, is non-toxic and lasts for several days in an airtight container.

Cornflour paste: (see page 8).

Extra strong homemade liquid starch: (see page 8).

Flour paste: (see page 8).

Homemade commercial-strength liquid starch: (see page 8).

Paper paste: cornflour paste or flour paste (see recipes page 8) can be used for papier-mâché or collage. **Commercial paper paste** is widely available.

PVA glue: stands for poly vinyl adhesive and is widely available.

Starch: (see page 8).

paint

When the type of paint is not specified but listed as 'paint', any sort of non-toxic paint will do. Always store in an airtight container. Have children wear aprons while painting and keep a bucket of soapy water and sponges on hand.

Fabric paint: is available from art, craft and department stores. Use when permanent prints on fabric are required. **Fabric crayons:** can be used to draw designs directly onto fabric.

Fingerpaint: any thick non-toxic paint can be used for fingerpainting. Fingerpaint can be made by adding powder paint, food colouring, vegetable dye or tempera paint to cornflour paste (see recipe page 8).

Food colouring: widely available in liquid form from supermarkets. It can be used as a substitute for vegetable dye, but the colours are paler. Food colouring also comes in a paste which is more intense in colour, but is more difficult to find.

Painting on foil and plastic: mix ½ cup of thick **powder paint** mixture with 1 teaspoon of dishwashing liquid. If the paint does not adhere, add another ½ teaspoon of dishwashing liquid. The dishwashing liquid makes the paint stick to glossy surfaces.

Powder paint: available in a variety of colours. Powder paint is an economical paint that is mixed with water. **Cornflour paste** can be added to the mixture to achieve a thicker consistency.

Powder tempera paint: available in a large variety of colours as a powder and also as a liquid. It is a flat opaque paint which is better suited for some art projects as it covers writing on boxes very well. Put powder in a container, add a little water to make a paste then add a little more to make paint. Liquid starch, **cornflour paste** or **paper paste** can be added to give it transparency and to increase volume as it can be expensive. It may rub off onto hands and clothing when dry. Thick paint sometimes cracks but adding paper paste helps to prevent this.

Thick paint: powder paint or **vegetable dye paint** can be mixed with cornflour to create a thicker consistency.

Thin paint: powder paint or **vegetable dye paint** can be diluted with water to create a thinner consistency.

Vegetable dye: is made by placing about 1 tablespoon of water in a container and adding ⅛ of a teaspoon of dye powder and stirring. Add more dye for a more intense colour. Vegetable dye can be purchased at children's educational toy stores. **Food colouring** can be used as a substitute.

Vegetable dye paint: made by dissolving about ⅛ of a teaspoon of **vegetable dye** powder in a tablespoon of water and adding it to **paper paste** or **starch**. The colours are most brilliant and translucent when mixed with commercial paper paste. It does not cover lettering on boxes or newsprint as well as **powder tempera paint**, which is an opaque paint.

unusual painting tools

Refillable roll-on deodorant containers filled with paint.
Feather duster used on a very large sheet of paper as a paintbrush.
Plastic squeeze bottles.
Shaving brushes.
Feathers.
Fly swatter.
Sponges.
End of a piece of cardboard.

printing techniques

Paint is applied to the object to be printed usually by three methods: painting the object with a brush; rolling over the object with a hard paint roller or print roller that has been covered with paint by rolling in a paint-filled tray; or by pressing the object onto a print pad. On page 9 we show you how to make a print pad.

clay

Natural clay is excellent for modelling. It is available from art and craft supplies stores, but buy it in solid form as it is messy to make up from powder. Pieces of clay can be sliced off a block of clay with string or wire tied to two empty thread reels. Interesting textures can be made by scraping or pressing objects into the clay. Children may want to save the clay objects they have moulded. Let the objects dry thoroughly and they can be painted or lacquered and glued onto a wooden base if desired. It is not advisable to fire the clay products of young children as any air bubbles trapped in the clay will explode and someone will be very disappointed. Clay that is to be fired must be kneaded until the air bubbles escape. Clay is a bit messy. The table top can be protected with a heavy garbage bag that has been cut open and taped down. This or any

similar material can be thrown out afterwards. Save all excess clay in an airtight container to prevent it drying out. If storing for more than a few days, press a thumb into each clay ball and fill hole with water. Clay can clog drains so scrape the excess into a storage container. Although the main purpose of clay is manual manipulation, every child should experience the delight of putting it through a garlic press!

collage & construction

Collage is artwork made from various materials glued, taped or stapled to a surface. Assorted collage materials include dyed pasta, chenille sticks (pipe cleaners), cellophane, magazine pages, crepe paper, leaves, flowers, seashells, wood shavings—the list is endless!

Crepe paper curls: cut ½cm (¼in) strips off the end of a roll of crepe paper. Cut through completely one end of strip and roll the strips between your palms to separate the unfolded papers.

how to dye collage materials

Matchsticks, toothpicks, iceblock sticks: place in a warm vegetable dye mixture. Wood colours more quickly in warm dye. Spread on newspaper to dry.

Paper: fill a baking dish with water and add vegetable dye or food colouring. Lay paper flat in the baking dish until completely submerged. Hang paper to dry. For best results use rice paper or a thin absorbent paper.

Pasta: wearing gloves, place food colouring or vegetable dye (start with ⅛ teaspoon) into cold water. Place pasta into the dye, swish it around and remove quickly before it becomes sticky. Spread on a thick wad of newspaper. As it is drying, run your hand over pasta to keep it from adhering to the newspaper.

safety first

Activities that involve small objects, such as polystyrene, beads and buttons should be kept for older children, over five years. There is a high risk that younger children will put these objects into their mouths, ears or noses.

Before buying or using craft materials check labels to ensure that all felt-tipped pens, crayons, play dough, paints and glues are non-toxic. Play dough can be made at home with edible dye (see play dough recipes on page 9).

Supervise children using scissors to avoid cuts and wounds. Make sure all scissors are put away after use. Choose scissors with a blunt end or children's safety scissors or training scissors.

Supervise all use of string and cord so that children do not use it to cut off circulation or breathing.

Older children only should use needles and these should be blunt-ended. Keep pins and needles in a secure container away from children. Make sure all pins and needles are put away after use to avoid nasty accidents.

Supervise all washing up of tools after use. Water is dangerous and children can drown in a small amount of water.

collecting & storing materials

These materials will be handy for collage, construction, painting, printing and many other children's crafts.

bark	confetti	foam pieces	mesh	plastic containers	sticks
beads & buttons	corks	fur	old clean socks	polystyrene pieces	straws
bottle tops	corrugated cardboard	greeting cards	old telephone books	rubber bands	string
boxes & containers	cotton reels	postcards	orange & onion bags	sandpaper	thread
cardboard sheets	cotton wool	hair curlers	paper & cardboard	seeds	wire
cellophane	cylinders	magazines	paper clips	shells	wire coat-hangers
chenille sticks	egg cartons	matchsticks	paper patty pans	springs	wood off-cuts
clock parts	fabric scraps	matchboxes	pasta (dry)	squirt & spray bottles,	wool

Store collage and craft materials in separate containers to avoid mixing them up. It can be a nightmare trying to separate hundreds of small items! Make collecting items fun and encourage children to think creatively about how they can expand their collections of collage and craft materials.

fingerpaint & glue recipes

cornflour paste

Add to ordinary paint or add food colouring to use as fingerpaint; use as an economical extender for paint; use as a paper glue or use in papier-mâché.

you will need
3 parts water (3 cups)
1 part cornflour (1 cup)
food colouring
saucepan

1   **Adult:** bring the water to boil in a saucepan. Remove from heat.
2   **Adult:** dissolve cornflour in a little cold water and add to hot water, stirring constantly. Boil until clear and thick (about one minute).

To make fingerpaint, add desired food colouring. This mixture will be very smooth. Offer it to the children while it is still warm to touch. A tablespoon of glycerine may be added to make it glossy. A ½ cup of Lux soap flakes may be added to give fingerpaint a lumpy texture.

Store in refrigerator as it spoils in hot weather.

flour paste

Useful for gluing collage and papier-mâché paper.

you will need
1 part water
1 part flour
food colouring
oil of cloves, wintergreen or peppermint
bowl
spoon

1   Pour water into bowl. Add flour, stirring constantly. Add food colouring. Salt may be added for a different texture.
2   Add a few drops of oil of cloves, wintergreen or peppermint as preservatives. Thin with cold water.

Store in airtight container in refrigerator. Longlasting.

starch

Very useful for gluing paper. It dries clear and sticks to glass, metal, waxed paper, plastics. Occasionally commercial-strength liquid starch is not thick enough.

you will need
1 part starch granules (1 cup)
2 parts boiling water (2 cups)
food colouring
saucepan

1   **Adult:** add a small amount of cold water (about 6 tablespoons) to starch granules to make a paste.
2   **Adult:** add boiling water to starch, stirring constantly. The mixture should become thick and milky glossy. If it doesn't thicken it is because the water isn't hot enough. Simply put it on the stove and bring it to the boil. Remove from stove.
3   Add food colouring. Add some glycerine to make mixture glossy and/or ½ cup of Lux soap flakes for a different texture. Give starch mixture to children while still warm.

Store in refrigerator as it spoils in hot weather.

homemade commercial-strength liquid starch
Dissolve 1 teaspoon of granulated starch in a small amount of water. While stirring, add 1 cup of hot water. Bring to the boil for one minute, stirring constantly. Cool.

Store in airtight container in refrigerator. Longlasting.

extra strong homemade liquid starch
Follow instructions for Homemade commercial-strength liquid starch (above), using 1 tablespoon of granulated starch instead of a teaspoon.

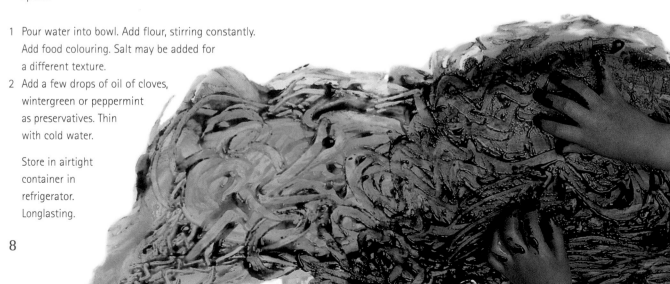

play dough recipes

play dough

you will need
1 cup salt
2 cups flour
4 teaspoons cream of tartar
2 tablespoons cooking oil
2 cups water
powder paint or vegetable dye or food colouring
saucepan

1 Mix all ingredients in saucepan.
2 **Adult:** cook on medium heat for three to five minutes, stirring constantly until mixture becomes stiff. Store in airtight container in refrigerator. It will last for quite a while and has the consistency of commercially prepared play dough. Additional colour may be worked into dough.

how to make a print pad

you will need
thin sponge
shallow tray

1 Place a sponge in the tray. Place several spoonsful of paint onto the sponge.
2 To print, just press the printing object onto the sponge. The sponge loads a minimum amount of paint, evenly distributed across the printing object, which helps to avoid smearing and gives a clear print. Make a cushion by placing a newspaper under the paper on which the print impression is to be made.

uncooked salt dough

This is the easiest recipe; it can be made in less than three minutes. Let children make the dough themselves whenever possible. This recipe makes enough for six children.

you will need
powder paint or vegetable dye or food colouring
2 cups flour
1 cup salt
1 tablespoon cooking oil
1 cup water
bowl
spoons

1 Mix powder paint or vegetable dye or food colouring with the flour and salt. Add oil and water.
2 Knead dough. Children will like to use rollers, biscuit cutters and toothpicks with dough. If it becomes sticky, add more flour. Dough will keep for more than a week, even longer if it is kept in the refrigerator but it has a tendency to crumble.

Small shapes of this mixture can be baked in a 180° C (350° F) oven for 45 minutes to make them hard.

tip Children will sometimes want to add more flour to play dough to make it seem like they are really bakers. Occasionally, leave the dough white so they can colour it themselves with powder paint in plastic salt shakers. Fragrances may be added to any of the dough mixtures. Let children mix different coloured dough together; this will give a marbled effect. Wash utensils used to make dough before it dries on them. Play dough will clog the drain so don't try to dispose of it by washing it away. Disinfectants and alum are sometimes added as preservatives but they are not necessary in recipes with a high salt content. Salt sometimes attracts moisture if dough is in a sealed container, so if the mixture is sticky, just add a little flour to get the right consistency.

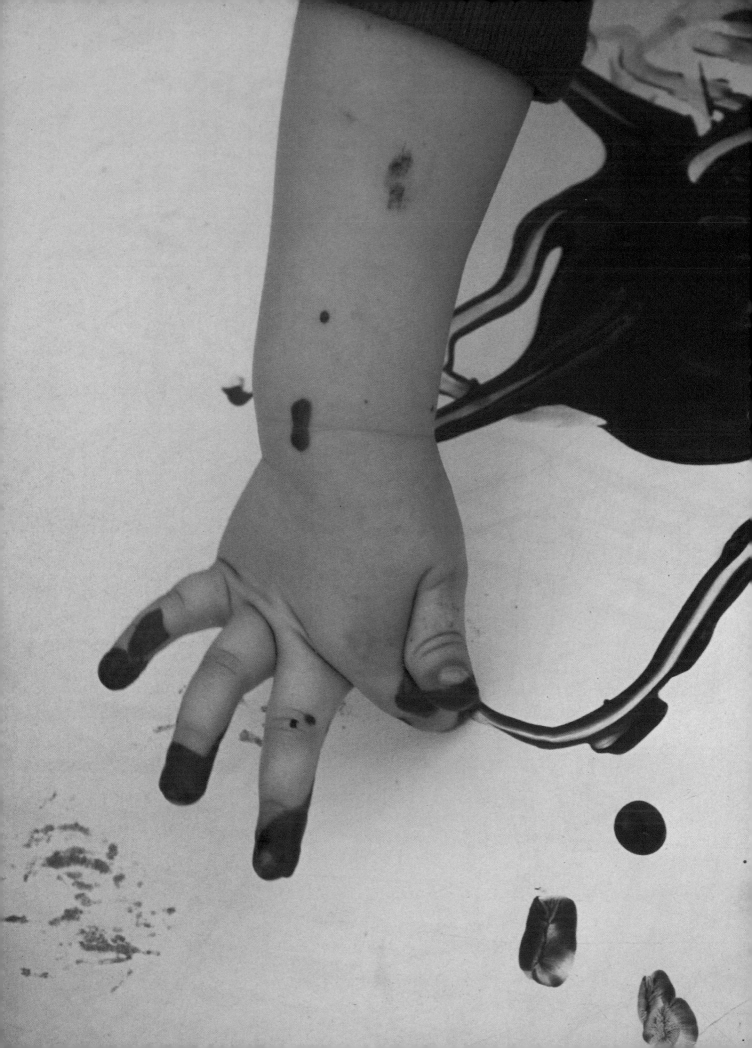

drawing &
painting

Children love the sensations of blending colour, texture and design. Experimenting with different types of paint—whether thick, thin, airy or glossy—or different drawing tools —wax or chalk crayons, cork, pencils or pens —can lead children on a sensory adventure. Encourage experimentation with colours, tools and designs, and let different techniques be combined to create delightful new effects.

11

creating different effects for drawing

Good quality felt-tipped pens give the greatest colour with good clarity of line. Unfortunately, these pens dry out easily, so must be kept capped.

Chalk colours are more vivid if the paper has been dampened with a sponge before drawing. Chalk also dries with more colour and a slight gloss when the paper has been brushed with evaporated milk or buttermilk before using the chalk.

Burnt cork can be used to create a charcoal effect on paper. An adult can burn the end of a long wine cork with a match or lighter. The child then draws on paper with the burnt end of the cork. When the burnt end wears off, the cork can be burnt again.

Coloured pencils, wax crayons and oil pastels are also good drawing tools for children to use.

ideas to stimulate children´s imaginations

Children enjoy making drawings from their initials and can produce the most imaginative interpretations. Another idea to inspire individual and original expression is for an adult to scribble on paper and let a young child turn the scribbles into people, animals, or space creatures, for instance. Turning objects upside down and drawing them provides another interesting perspective. Children will more readily try a new interpretation (rather than reproducing the object accurately) if the object is treated differently or becomes unusual.

OVER
3
YEARS

fingerprint drawings

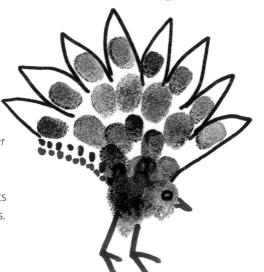

you will need
child's ink pad
sheet of paper
felt-tipped pen

1 Gently place finger on stamp pad so that finger is well-covered with ink. Carefully press finger on paper ensuring that finger does not move and smudge the ink. Allow prints to dry.
2 Draw features on a single print or several fingerprints to make them into creatures, birds, flowers or insects.

magic drawing

you will need
liquid bleach
cotton buds
coloured tissue paper or
   white paper painted all
   over with thin paint
sheet of paper
small bowl

1 **Adult:** put about 1 tablespoon of bleach in bowl. Replace bleach lid and put up on shelf out of reach of children.

2 Put end of cotton bud into bleach and then place that end onto tissue paper and draw a picture. Within a few seconds the area that has been touched with bleach will turn a paler colour or white. Darker colours may need more bleach. The disappearance of colour on tissue paper shows up better when a sheet of white paper is placed directly underneath.

Safety first
Ensure that bleach does not come in contact with skin.
Keep lid on bleach and keep it out of reach of children at all times.

Place your magic drawing over white or brightly coloured cardboard or paper to make unusual cards or wrapping paper.

ALL AGES

fabric designs

you will need
fabric crayons (see page 4)
white drawing paper
fabric (synthetic or a blend of
    polyester/cotton)
sheet of paper, if needed
iron

1 **Adult:** carefully read directions accompanying fabric crayons.
2 Using fabric crayons, draw a design or picture on the drawing paper
   on one side of the paper only. (Please note that the design will be
   reversed when transferred to the fabric.) Cut out the design.
3 **Adult:** following directions included in fabric crayons packet,
   transfer the design from paper to fabric. (If you are using a T-shirt
   or pillowcase, place plain paper inside to stop dye going through to
   fabric underneath.) Place design, right-side down on top of fabric.
   Take care not to move the design or a double image will result. Move
   iron evenly across design to prevent steam marks appearing on fabric.
   If the iron is left in the same spot for too long, colour will not result
   where the iron's steam holes have been sitting above the fabric.

personal book

you will need
1 metre (about 1 yard) calico
sewing thread and needle
children's favourite drawings
clear self-adhesive plastic
shoe laces, wool or embroidery cotton
fabric pen
sewing pins
hole puncher
scissors

1 **Adult:** cut calico into equal-sized rectangular shapes. This will be the size of the book when it is open.
2 Place rectangular shapes on top of each other. Fold material in half and mark the centre (the spine) with sewing pins. Hand sew, with colourful thread, a seam down the centre to hold pages firmly together.
3 Cut out favourite drawings.
4 Cover the drawings with self-adhesive plastic. Punch hole in the top of drawings.
5 Attach shoe laces, wool or cotton to book pages by sewing them into place or threading them through two small cuts made in the fabric. The drawings may then be tied into the book with shoe laces or wool or cotton lengths.
6 Captions may be written on each page with a fabric pen. Children can move the drawings around from page to page to suit the story they want to tell.

A personal book is a wonderful way to preserve favourite drawings and to help children learn to tie things.

OVER 4 YEARS

crayon etchings

you will need
crayons (light colours)
small sheet of paper
newspaper
black crayon or thick black
   powder paint (see page 5)
   in small bowl
hairpin or end of a paintbrush

1 Pressing firmly to produce a thick layer of crayon, cover all the paper with different coloured crayons. Place a thick pad of newspaper under the sheet of paper. Cover crayon picture with black crayon or black powder paint. Allow to dry. The newspaper pad helps the black crayon to cover the paper more evenly but remove the newspaper pad for the etching, which requires a hard surface.

2 Place paper on one layer of newspaper (to make clean-up easier). Make another picture by scraping off the black layer of paint or crayon with the end of a hairpin or end of paintbrush to reveal colours underneath. (Any blunt instrument can be used to scrape off the black layer. Use different blunt instruments for different effects.)

magic painting

you will need
sheet of absorbent paper
long thin candle
thin paint in small bowl
brushes (shaving brushes are easy
    for small children to hold)
apron

1 Put on apron.
2 Draw on absorbent paper using
  either end of the candle
  depending on the desired effect.
3 Paint over the wax design using
  a brush and one or more colours.
  The wax design resists the paint
  and shows through clearly.

Try using crayons instead of
candles; black is most effective.

The wax design appears just like magic!

easel painting

you will need
clothes pegs, bull-dog clips
  or adhesive tape
large sheet of paper
easel
paint in small bowls
long-handled paintbrushes
apron

1 **Adult:** peg, clip or tape the
   paper onto the easel.
2 Put on apron. Using lots
   of different colours, paint
   pictures on the paper.
4 Remove paper from easel and
   allow it to dry thoroughly.

tip Long-handled paintbrushes allow
     more freedom of movement,
     although short-handled brushes
     are much easier for younger
     children to use. When buying or
     making an easel, make sure the
     paint tray has an opening
     which makes cleaning easier.
     Sometimes a paint stand is more
     suitable. Two easels placed next
     to each other encourages
     interaction between children.

mural painting

you will need

masking tape or bull-dog clips
length of heavyweight paper
   (more than 1 metre
   [1 yard] wide) — an end roll of
   heavyweight paper is
   often available, free of
   charge, from newspaper
   publishers or printers.
fence, brick wall or easel
paint in small bowls
paintbrushes
apron

1 **Adult:** tape or clip paper along a fence or a brick wall,
   or tape or clip the paper onto an easel.
2 Put on apron. Paint pictures on paper. Mural painting
   is a fun group activity, especially at parties.

Make up your own play
and use the mural as
back-drop scenery. Cut
into sections, tape to a
wall and change it each
time for different acts.

spray-paint mural

you will need
masking tape or bull-dog clips
length of heavyweight paper
   (more than 1 metre
   [1 yard] wide)—an end roll of
   heavyweight paper is
   often available, free of
   charge, from newspaper
   publishers or printers.
brick wall, fence or easel
thin paint in red, yellow and blue
spray bottles
apron

1 **Adult:** tape or clip paper along
   a fence, a brick wall or tape or
   clip the paper onto an easel.
   Pour paint into spray bottles.
2 Put on apron. Squirt the paint
   onto paper. Colours will mix
   and overlap, creating various
   patterns on the paper.

A spray-paint mural is a colourful party activity and makes a beautiful decoration.

straw painting

you will need
non-absorbent paper
newspaper
food colouring mixed with water,
   or thin paint
spoon or paintbrush
straws
apron

1 Put on apron.
2 Place paper on newspaper-covered
   table. Put a little paint or food colouring
   on paper with spoon or paintbrush.
3 Point straw in direction you want paint
   to go; put straw to lips and blow. The
   paint will fan out to make interesting
   patterns the more you blow on the
   straw. (Remember not to breathe in.)

powder painting

you will need
liquid starch
sheet of paper
paintbrushes
powder paint
apron

1 Put on apron.
2 Pour a puddle of starch onto
   paper. Spread starch over
   paper with paintbrush.
3 With another slightly damp
   paintbrush, pick up the paint
   powder and dab onto starch-
   covered paper. The powder will
   dissolve and become thick paint,
   creating a pleasing texture.

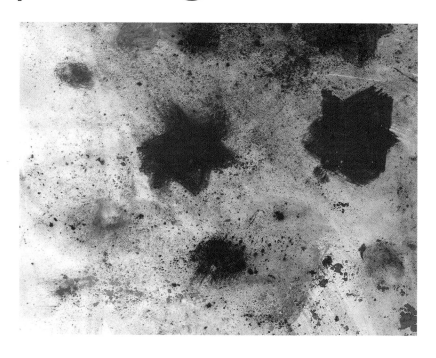

string painting

OVER 4 YEARS

you will need

sheet of paper, folded in half
paint in shallow dishes
50cm (20in) lengths of string
apron

1 Put on apron.

2 Place pre-folded piece of paper beside paint tray. Open paper.

3 Drop one end of string into paint, keeping hold of dry end.

4 Pull string out of tray onto paper until paint-covered string
  is on paper and dry end of the string is at the edge of paper.

5 While still holding onto the string, carefully fold the paper
  on top of the string with your free hand.

6 Press down on paper and pull string out. Open paper.

7 Repeat with a new string dipped in a different colour. (Use
  separate strings for each colour.) For a different design, drag the
  string sideways around the paper while pulling it out.

After gaining a little experience with this method, try using thick
and thin paint and mix it with some glue for a different effect.

ALL AGES

body painting

you will need

sheet of paper, larger than
   the child

crayons

paint in small bowls

paintbrushes

scissors

apron

1 Put on apron.

2 Place paper on floor. Child should lie face up on top of paper.

3 Using a crayon, draw an outline around the child's whole body.

4 Colour in body drawn on paper with crayons or paint.
   Older children might like to create a series of characters.

5 Finished figures can be cut out and used for further play.
   This activity encourages development of a positive self-image.

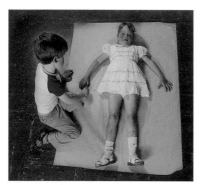

Ask a friend to draw an outline around you.

Use different colours for different body parts.

Carefully cut around the body shape.

It is also great fun to 'dress' the cut-out shape of yourself or other characters with old clothes or fabric scraps.

bubble painting

Remember not to breathe in the paint!

you will need
dishwashing liquid
powder tempera paint
  or powder paint
straws
sheet of paper
empty cans or plastic
  containers
water
apron

1 Put on apron.
2 Pour ¼ cup of dishwashing liquid into container. In a separate container, mix small amount of water with paint.
3 Add paint mixture to dishwashing liquid until colour is intense.
4 Practise blowing on a straw.
5 Put straw into paint mixture and gently blow until the bubbles slightly flow over the top of the container. (Do not breath the paint in through the straw).
6 Roll paper around gently on top of bubbles so as not to burst the bubbles. Try not to press the paper flat on top of the bubbles. Repeat the process with several colours for a pretty sheet of multi-coloured paper.
7 Allow paper to dry before using.

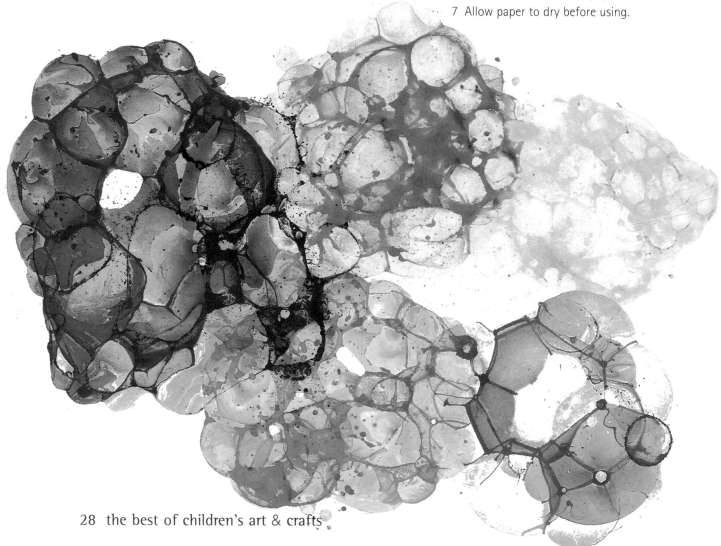

blot painting

Apply the paint close to the fold line.

Open out the paper to admire the effect.

you will need
sheet of paper
paint in small bowls
spoon or paintbrush
apron

1 Put on apron.
2 Fold paper in half. Open it out. Very young
   children will need the paper to be pre-folded.
3 Spoon or brush the paint out in drops onto
   paper, mainly along the central fold line.
4 Re-fold paper. Rub paper with palm of hand
   from fold out to the edge of the paper.

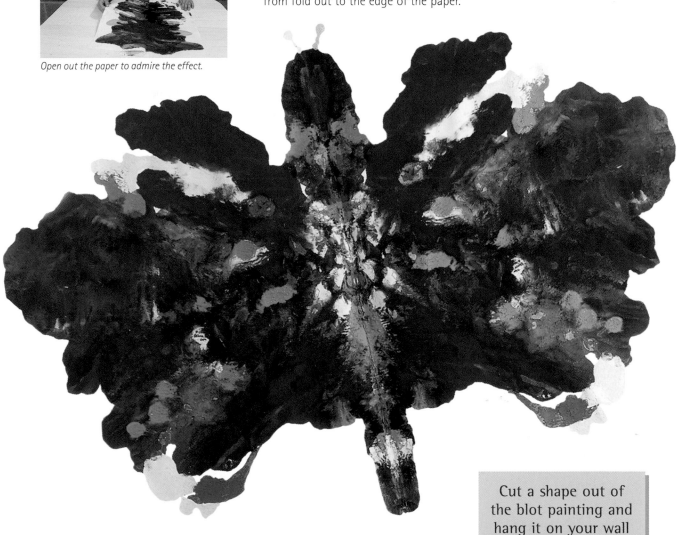

Cut a shape out of
the blot painting and
hang it on your wall
as a decoration.

ALL AGES

marble painting

you will need
marbles
paint in small bowls
sheet of paper
large cardboard box
straining spoon
bowls of water
apron

1 Put on apron.
2 Place marbles in paint bowls. Place paper in bottom of box.
3 Spoon a coloured marble into the box. Roll the marble
   around so that it leaves a coloured pattern on the
   paper. Take marble out with spoon and wash it in one of the
   bowls of water. Repeat with different coloured marbles.
4 Take the painting out of the box and hang to dry.

window painting

Powder paint is recommended because it wipes easily off windows and has the most intense colours. Soap paint and any paint mixed with white liquid shoe polish are also suitable. Paste- and starch-based paint is hard to wash off windows.

you will need
newspapers
powder paint mixed in
   small bowls
paintbrushes
adhesive tape
apron

1 Put on apron.
2 Tape newspaper to bottom of window and floor to protect floor and ledges from paint.
3 Paint onto inside of window as rain will wash off any outside painting. Paintings can be left for days or weeks.
4 Wash painting off with sponge and soapy water. The paint does not mark window in any way but the longer it is left, the harder it is to remove as it seems to bake on.

Some window paintings are so pretty you'll wish they'd last forever.

OVER
3
YEARS

crayon-resist painting

you will need

sheet of paper

crayons

tempera powder paint mixed in
    small bowl

paintbrush

apron

Tempera powder paint gives the most dramatic
result because of its opaque quality.

1 Put on apron.
2 Pressing down firmly, draw a design on the paper
   with different coloured crayons.
3 Cover drawing with the paint. The best results occur
   when light-coloured crayons are used with dark paint
   or dark-coloured crayons are used with light paint.

sponge painting

you will need
small sponge pieces
clothes pegs
paint, small amounts in shallow trays
sheet of paper
apron

1 Put on apron.
2 Hold sponge pieces with a peg.
3 Dip sponge into the paint and use it to dab or brush paint onto the paper making pictures and patterns.
4 Keep the sponge pieces in their original paint tray to avoid mixing colours. It also helps to colour match the peg with the paint, for example, a blue peg with the blue paint, etc.

Repeatedly dabbing the sponge onto the paper can create striking geometrical effects.

Using the sponge as a brush is a great way to colour large spaces.

OVER
4
YEARS

monster painting

Use lots of different coloured paints and allow them to mix and run together.

you will need
thin paint in small bowls
paintbrushes or rollers
sheet of paper
felt-tipped pens
apron

1 Put on apron.
2 Paint over the paper with several different colours.
3 Allow the colours to mix and run together all over the paper.
4 Hang painting to dry.
5 Ask an adult to help you find monsters in the painting. Outline monsters using a felt-tipped pen.

roller painting

Dab, swirl, circle or drag the roller. What other roller techniques can you think of to use?

you will need
foam rollers, preferably small
thin paint in shallow trays
paper, absorbent not shiny
apron

1 Put on apron.
2 Dip the roller into the paint and spread the paint, trying different techniques, for example, waves or stripes. Repeat with different colours. Encourage children to replace rollers in original colour containers as paint blends quickly.

fingerpainting

you will need

fingerpaint (see page 8 for recipe),
  1 to 3 colours in bowls
    with large spoon
laminated tabletop
grout scrapers (from hardware store)
plastic combs
apron

1 Put on apron.
2 Spoon the fingerpaint onto the tabletop. Spread paint with hands to mix colours and enjoy the sensory experience. Draw patterns and pictures with hands and fingers, moving them all over the tabletop.

An excellent extension activity for older children is to use grout scrapers and combs to make patterns in the paint. Patterns can be made by scraping in straight lines or swirling movements.

There's no need to be too careful when applying the paint before fingerpainting.

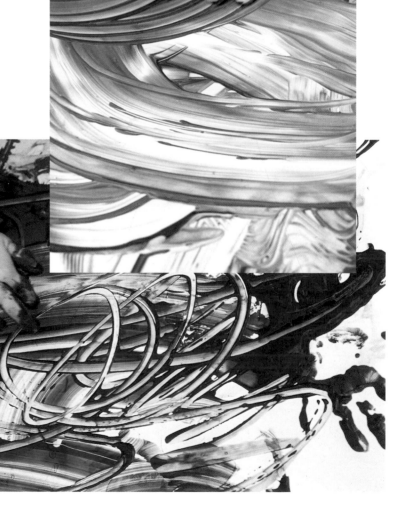

Dragging a grout scraper or comb through the paint creates attractive wavy patterns.

cleaning up

Have a large dish of warm, soapy water at the ready for paint-soaked hands. Remove aprons as soon as painting is finished to avoid getting paint on clothing. Some children may be reluctant to use fingerpaint. They may prefer to use a roller to spread the paint and a cautious fingertip to paint patterns. Emphasise that fingerpainting isn't dirty.

printing

A print is an impression of an object on fabric, paper or another surface. Printing encourages appreciation of texture and the development of design through the use of repetition. Children are also fascinated by the pattern reversal that occurs with printing. Because small muscle co-ordination is not necessary to achieve great results, young children experience a sense of accomplishment. And remember, the world is full of interesting shapes and objects —tennis balls, foam, leaves, flowers, fruit and vegetables, make the most wonderful prints.

OVER 3 YEARS

marbling

you will need
large polystyrene trays
waterproof ink, various colours
plastic spoons
light-coloured blotting paper
apron

1 Put on apron.
2 Half fill trays with water and gently spoon small amounts of ink onto surface of water. Stir mixture very carefully and slowly.
3 The ink will float, swirl and ooze to form fascinating patterns.
4 Place blotting paper on top of floating colours for 30 seconds. Quickly lift paper off, turn over, and immediately hold horizontally to stop ink running. Allow paper to dry on a flat surface.

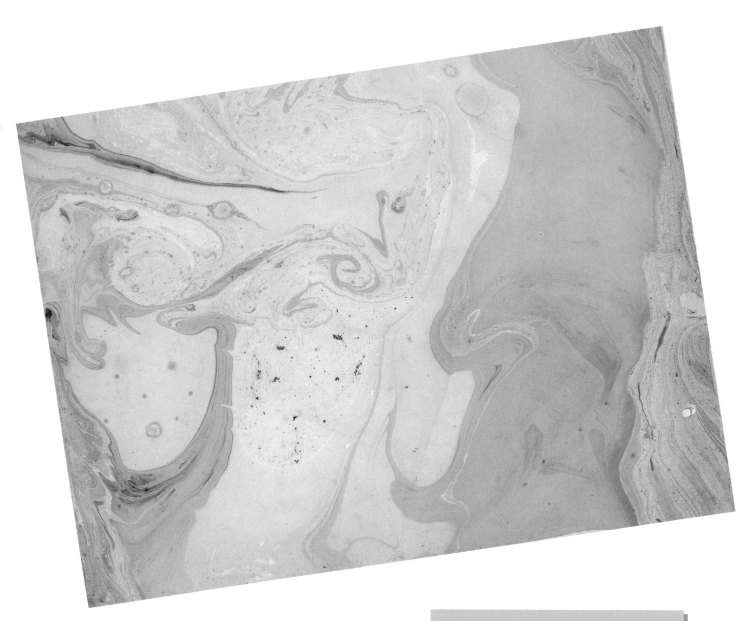

Marbling on thin absorbent paper looks striking taped to a window.

mesh dab-prints

you will need
plastic mesh bag (onion bags
    or pantihose)
foam, fibre filling or fabric scraps
print pads loaded with paint
    (see page 9)
paper
string
apron

1 **Adult:** make dabbers by filling
   plastic mesh squares or pantihose
   with foam, fibre or fabric scraps.
   Tie firmly with string.
2 Put on apron.
3 Press the dabber onto the foam
   print pad. Press dabber onto
   the paper. To avoid paint
   colours mixing, return dabbers
   to their original print pad.

*Dabbers make easy-to-hold printing
tools for young children.*

tennis ball prints

Remember to return each tennis ball to the
correct bowl so as not to mix the paints.

Dab or roll balls, and if you drop them be
careful not to splatter paint everywhere.

you will need
tennis balls (one for each paint colour)
thin paint in shallow bowls
sheet of paper
apron

1 Put on apron.
2 Dip tennis ball in paint. Dab, roll or drop ball on paper to make print.
3 Repeat the process with each different colour. Remember to keep
   balls in their original paint bowls to avoid mixing colours.
4 Hang or lay the prints flat to dry. If prints are hung, the paint tends
   to run and adds interesting patterns to the design. If you want clear
   splatter prints leave the prints to dry on a flat surface.

Use Christmas colours to
print festive wrapping paper.

42 the best of children's art & crafts

leaf prints

you will need
leaves
cardboard
PVA glue
thin paint
shallow dish (about 1cm
    [3/8in] deep)
print roller
sheet of absorbent paper
spoon
apron

Make sure the paint evenly coats the roller.

1 Put on apron.
2 Arrange leaves in desired
   design on the cardboard.
   Glue leaves onto cardboard
   and allow to dry.
3 Put a spoonful of paint into
   shallow dish. Move print roller
   through paint until roller is
   evenly coated. Roll paint onto
   leaves (a brush will not work).
4 Lay a piece of paper on top of
   the leaves. Rub the paper with
   a clean, dry hand. The raised
   veins and edges will make an
   impressive design. Take several
   prints from the same painting.

The same technique can be
used with wire mesh, lace or
netting instead of leaves.

play dough prints

you will need
play dough (see page 9)
tools (pencils, bottle caps, wire mesh,
    biscuit cutters, cooking utensils)
paint
print pad (see page 9)
paper

1 Roll play dough into a ball. Flatten
   it until it is about 5cm (2in) thick.
2 On one side of the play dough, press
   any tools in to make a design. You
   can also draw on the play dough with a
   pencil or the end of a paintbrush.
3 Gently press play dough onto print pad,
   remove, press onto paper. Repeat
   with different colours and designs.

fingerpainting prints

you will need

fingerpaint (see page 8)

table top (preferably laminated)

bucket of warm soapy water

large sheet of paper

towel

apron

1 Put on apron.

2 Put a small puddle of fingerpaint onto table top.

3 Fingerpaint on table top. When finished, wash hands in bucket of warm soapy water and dry them thoroughly with the towel.

4 Place a large sheet of paper on top of the fingerpainting. Carefully rub back of paper all over with clean, dry hands. Lift one side of paper print and slowly peel paper print off table top. Hang print up to dry.

Prints can also be made of pictures painted on the table top.

Fingerpainting is wonderful for releasing children's tension and anger while developing their hand-eye co-ordination.

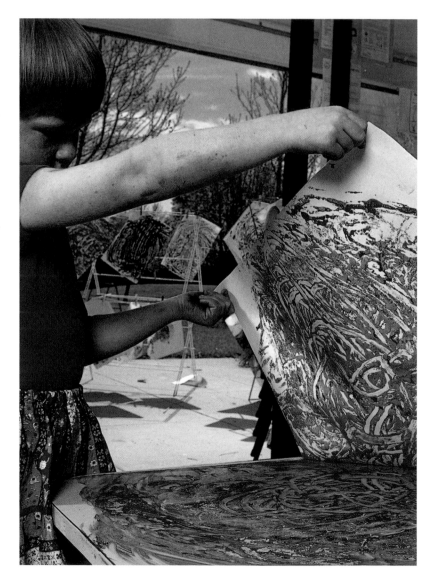

Place paper on fingerpainting, then place hands in the centre of paper and rub hands out to the edges without moving the paper.

OVER
3
YEARS

fruit & vegetable prints

you will need
oranges, lemons, potatoes,
  carrots, onions
paint
print pads (see page 9)
sheet of paper
knife
apron

1 **Adult:** cut fruit and vegetables in half to make a flat surface. Sometimes a fruit or vegetable must be allowed to drain upside down on a paper towel before it is able to absorb paint from the pad.
2 Put on apron.
3 Press printing object into print pad, remove, press onto paper. Repeat with different colours and different fruit and vegetables.

Hand prints can also be made by pressing hand onto print pad and then onto paper. Children over five may be able to cut a pattern into a potato with a plastic knife, spoon or melon scoop to get an unusual print on paper.

spatter stencil

you will need

large cardboard box, if necessary
sheet of paper
adhesive tape, if necessary
pressed leaves, flowers or stencils
    cut out of cardboard
comb or piece of wire screen
    taped to an old picture frame
    or a box screen
old toothbrush or nail brush
thin paint in bowl
apron

1 Put on apron.
2 If working in a restricted space, or in the house where furniture may get damaged, get a large grocery box and cut out one side. Place sheet of paper inside box and tape edges down so that it will not shift.
3 Lay leaves, flowers, grasses or stencils on paper.
4 Hold comb or place piece of wire screen about 10cm (4in) above level of paper. Our photograph is of a box screen made for preschool or kindergarten use. It is easy to improvise with an old picture frame.
5 Dip toothbrush or nail brush into paint.
6 Draw the paint-filled brush many times across the flat side of the comb or across the screen. If the brush is loaded with paint, spatter drops will be big and coarse. A small amount of paint will produce a spray effect.
7 Allow paint to dry, then remove leaves and other decorations.

For a different effect, try the spatter technique by scraping a piece of chalk over a screen held above glue or starch-covered paper.

The more paint that is loaded onto the brush, the thicker and coarser the spatter effect.

Wait until the paint dries completely before you remove the screen and the stencils.

fish prints

you will need
fresh dead fish with large scales (flat if possible)
newspaper
thin paint
paintbrush
absorbent paper, cut to size (blotting paper works well)
apron

1 Put on apron.

2 Lay fish on newspaper. Dry the fish with paper towels if it is still damp.
Paint one side of fish all over.

3 Carefully place absorbent paper on painted side of fish. With flat, dry
hand, press paper onto painted fish, taking care not to move paper.
Lift paper off and allow the print to dry. Several prints may be taken
each time the fish is painted. The first print is not always successful
if there is too much paint on the fish.

4 More colourful results can be achieved by two means. The first is to
paint different parts of the fish different colours before applying the
paper. The second is to follow steps 1 and 2, then paint the fish a
second, different colour and overprint fish onto the first dried print.

tips After a thorough cleaning, the fish is still perfectly good to eat.
You can use these same techniques with other types of seafood;
prawns give a particularly good result.

Spread the paint evenly over one side of fish.

Make several prints each time fish is painted.

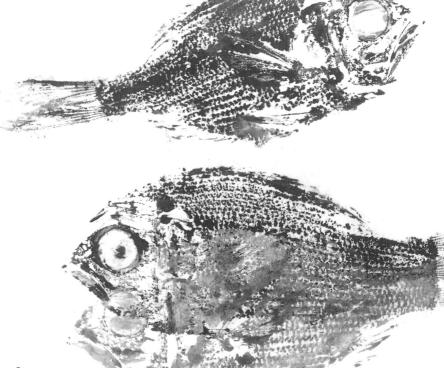

foam prints

you will need
thick foam
paint-loaded
   print pads (see page 9)
paper
scissors
apron

1 **Adult**: using scissors, cut thick foam into shapes. Shapes could be Christmas symbols, Easter eggs, geometric patterns, animals or letters. Older children can cut out their own printing shapes.
2 Put on apron. Press foam shape onto print pad then onto paper to make a print. Continue printing, using different colours and shapes until you are satisfied with the effect.
4 Hang prints to dry. Wash paint from foam shapes.

To make a print, press thick foam shape onto print pad then press foam onto paper.

Use different foam shapes and different colours to create different visual effects.

sponge prints

you will need
small thick sponges
clothes pegs
paint-loaded print pads (see page 9)
sheet of paper
scissors
apron

1 **Adult:** cut sponges into various shapes. Cut two slots in top of sponge, about 1cm (³/₈in) deep and 3cm (1¼in) apart, for peg to clip into. Clip peg into slots in top of sponge to act as a handle. Two thin sponges can be glued together with PVA glue and used in the same way.
2 Put on apron.
3 Press sponge onto printing pad, then press sponge onto paper. Repeat process with different shapes and colours. This creates a very interesting textual effect.

foot prints

you will need
paint
large baking dish
heavy sheet of paper
  (about 2 metres [about
  6½ft] long)
rocks
bucket of water and soap
spoon
towel

1 Using a spoon, spread a thin layer of paint over the bottom of the baking dish.
2 Lay paper on grass. Weigh down its edges with rocks to stop wind blowing paper. Place baking dish at one end of paper and bucket of water and towel at other end.
3 Step into baking dish then walk along paper, making different patterns. When at the other end, step into bucket of water and wash feet with soap. Dry with towel. Children may need to hold someone's hand while stepping from baking dish to paper, and from paper to the bucket.
4 Change colour in baking dish and repeat. Replace piece of paper before painting becomes too wet and slippery.
note If only lightweight paper is available or if the paper tears when it is trodden on, place paper on a concrete path.

string block prints

you will need
string or rope
small block of wood
paint in shallow tray (about 1 cm [³/₈in] deep)
sheet of paper
paintbrush
apron

1 Put on apron.
2 Wrap string around wooden block several times (making sure there is not a build up of string in one spot), and tie string in place at top of block.
2 Press string block into paint tray or paint string with paintbrush.
3 Make a print by placing string block on paper and pressing. Move block around in different directions until an interesting print design is created.

Wrap the string around the block several times so that interesting lines are formed.

printed doll

you will need

printing surface such as a
  laminated board, ceramic tile,
  heavy plastic or thick glass
pencil
fabric paint
paintbrushes
2 pieces of cotton fabric
needle and sewing thread or
  sewing machine
polyester fibre filling
raffia or wool for hair
fabric glue
ribbon
buttons, if desired
felt scraps, if desired
scissors
pins
apron

1 Put on apron.

2 On printing surface, draw a pencil outline of doll so both sides of doll are
   same shape. Paint picture of the front of the doll on the printing surface.

4 Place a fabric piece over the painted design and press gently with an open
   hand. Try not rub the fabric because the paint will smear.

5 Lift the fabric carefully, without moving it sideways. Hang the print to
   dry. Clean and dry the printing surface and paint a back view of the doll.
   Make a second print and leave to dry. Iron both fabric pieces (according
   to the paint manufacturer's instructions) to fix the paint.

6 Place both fabric pieces together and cut out around the doll, leaving
   a 2cm-wide (¾in) allowance. Avoid having very narrow sections of
   fabric as these will be difficult to fill with the fibre.

7 **Adult:** pin the two fabric pieces together with the printed sides to
   the inside. Stitch around the shape with a needle and thread, or sewing
   machine, and using a 2cm-wide (¾in) seam. At the top of the doll, leave
   a 10cm (4in) opening in the stitching to insert the fibre filling.

8 Turn through to right side and fill with fibre filling. Stitch opening closed.

9 Take a length of raffia or wool strands and plait each end, leaving an
   unplaited section in the centre. Glue the unplaited section onto the
   doll's head to make hair, leaving the plaits free. Tie the plaits with ribbon.
   Sew or glue on buttons for eyes and a felt nose, if desired.

Carefully paint within the pencil outline of the doll so that both sides are the same shape.

Ask someone to help you place the fabric over the painting so the print doesn't smudge.

With the palm of your hand, gently press, but do not rub, the fabric onto the painting.

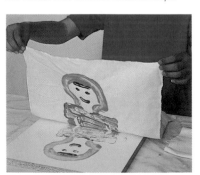

Slowly peel the fabric off the doll painting without lifting the fabric sideways.

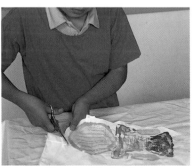

Cut around the edge of both doll shapes leaving at least a 2cm-wide (¾in) allowance.

An adult will need to sew the two sides together, then you can add the hair.

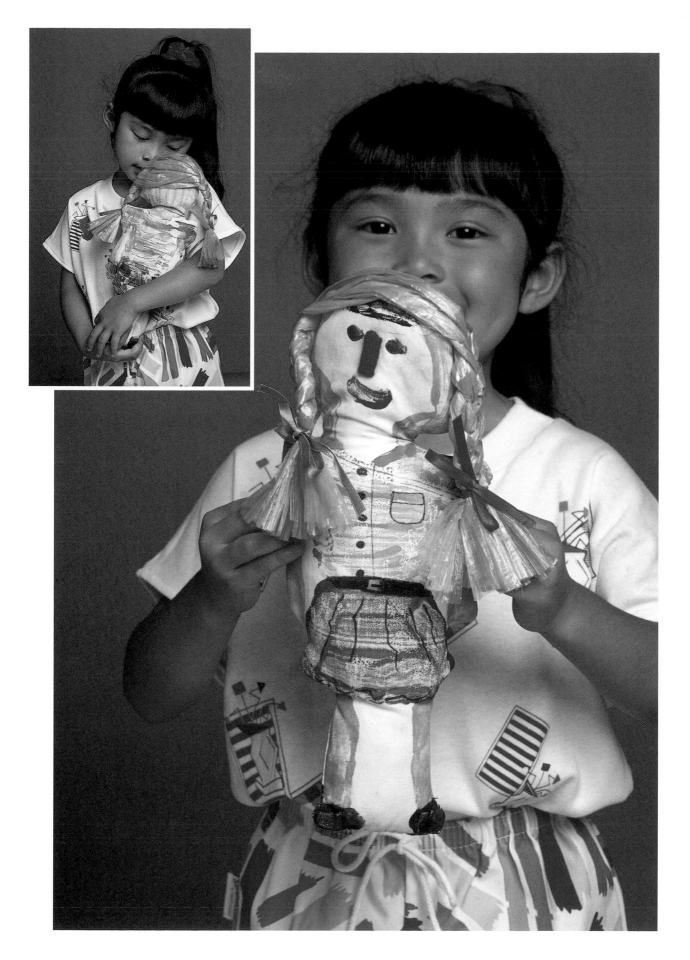

spool prints

you will need
paint-loaded print
  pads (see page 9)
spools of various shapes
  and sizes
sheet of paper
apron

1 Put on apron.
2 Press the spool onto print pad,
   then press the spool onto paper.
   Continue printing using different
   spools and different colours.

Young children will love the feeling of using spools of different shapes and sizes.

Glue the spool prints
onto cardboard and
cover with clear self-
adhesive plastic to make
bright placemats.

kitchen gadget prints

OVER
3
YEARS

you will need
kitchen gadgets such as ice
    block trays, strainers, whisks,
    containers, biscuit cutters, and
    any gadget with an interesting
    shape and a flat surface
paint-loaded print
    pads (see page 9)
large sheets of paper
apron

1 Put on apron.
2 Press printing gadget onto print
   pad. Stamp gadget onto paper to
   make a print. Continue printing
   with different objects and colours
   until the print is complete.

*Whisks of all shapes and sizes make great
printing gadgets and they're also fun to use.*

*Try printing on different coloured paper for
striking and colourful effects.*

OVER
5
YEARS

crayon screen prints

The lines of the design need to be quite thick so draw over the design a couple of times.

Lay the fabric or garment flat and smooth out creases before you place the screen on top.

Ask a friend to hold the screen while you drag the squeegee across the screen surface.

Ask a friend to hold down the fabric or garment while you gently lift the screen.

you will need
oil pastel crayons
silk screen
fabric or garment
   (for printing)
fabric paint
squeegee
cleaning rag
mineral turpentine
spoon
apron

1 Put on apron.
2 Using crayons draw a design directly onto the mesh of the screen.
3 Draw over the design again until the crayon lines are quite thick.
   If printing a garment place paper between front and back to avoid paint
   soaking through both layers of fabric. Place fabric or garment undernea
   the screen and spread fabric so there are no creases. Spoon a thick strip
   paint along one side of the screen. If using more than one colour, spoon
   strips of paint alongside each other being careful not to overlap the pai
4 Have an adult or friend hold the screen firmly. Drag the squeegee acros
   the screen surface, spreading paint evenly. Repeat two or three times.
5 Have an adult or friend hold the fabric or garment. Carefully lift screen,
   raising it from one side to the other. Remove excess paint from the scre
6 **Adult:** saturate a rag with mineral turpentine and scrub the crayon
   pattern off the screen. Wash the screen thoroughly with cool water.
7 Hang the fabric or garment to dry. Before wearing or washing, iron the
   fabric (according to paint manufacturer's instructions) to fix the paint.

roller prints

you will need

foam shapes, wool, string or tyre inner tube

cardboard cylinder

thick paint-loaded print pad (see page 9)

large sheet of paper

PVA glue

apron

1 Put on apron.

2 Glue foam shapes, wool, string or tyre inner tube around the cardboard cylinder.

3 Roll cardboard cylinder onto foam print pad. Then roll the cylinder over the paper. Repeat the print until the paper is covered.

Roller-printed patterns make attractive gift-wrapping paper.

Arrange the foam shapes and objects so that there is a uniform space between them.

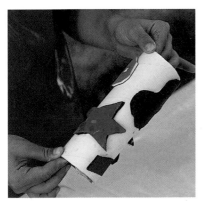

Use lots of different shapes to create a striking visual pattern.

Roll the cylinder on the print pad, making sure the paint evenly coats the shapes.

Carefully roll the cardboard cylinder without rubbing the paint off the shapes.

printing 57

dyeing

Dyeing is an easy way to colour fabric. Results are quick, often spectacular and give a sense of satisfaction and accomplishment—a boost to any child's self-esteem. Children love exploring colour blending and discovering new dyeing effects. They'll be thrilled with their results such as wall hangings, tablecloths, cushion covers and T-shirts.

dip & dye

you will need
2 or 3 vegetable dyes or cold-water fabric dyes
2 or 3 buckets or large ice-cream containers
cotton fabric
rubber gloves
apron

1 Put on apron.
2 **Adult:** mix the vegetable or fabric dyes in separate buckets or containers according to the manufacturer's instructions.
3 Fold the fabric several times to make a small triangle or square.
4 Put on rubber gloves. Dip each corner of the folded fabric into a different coloured dye. Allow the dyes to meet in the centre of the fabric. Squeeze out excess dye after each application.
5 Open out the fabric. Hang to dry.

Gently dip a corner of the fabric into the dye and allow the excess dye to drip off.

Dip the fabric into the second colour so that it overlaps the edges of the first colour.

Dyed fabric makes a terrific cushion cover, tablecloth or a striking wall hanging.

reverse
dip & dye

you will need

liquid bleach

bucket or large ice-cream
  container

dark-coloured cotton fabric
  (black, dark blue and blue
  denim work well)

rubber gloves

apron

1 Put on apron.
2 **Adult:** pour bleach into the bucket or ice-cream container.
3 Fold the fabric several times to make a small triangle or square.
4 Put on rubber gloves. Dip each corner of the folded fabric into
   bleach. Hold each corner in the bleach until it changes colour.
5 Open out fabric. Hang to dry.

Safety first
Ensure that bleach does not come in contact with skin. Keep lid
on bleach and keep it out of children's reach at all times.

*Dip fabric into bleach until the fabric changes
colour, then allow excess bleach to drip off.*

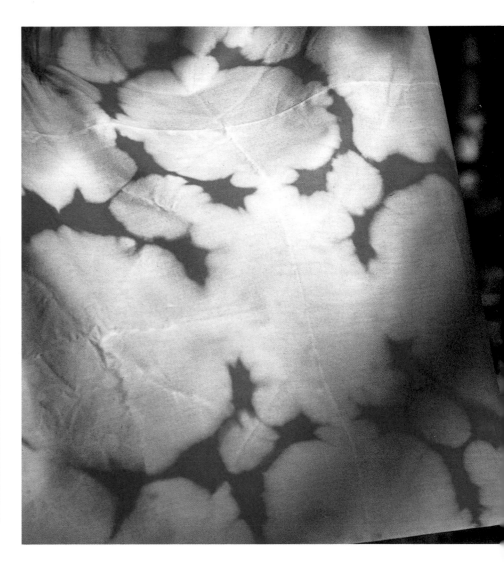

OVER
6
YEARS

multi-coloured tie-dyeing

you will need

2 or 3 vegetable dyes or cold-
   water fabric dyes
2 or 3 buckets or large ice-cream
   containers
white cotton garment or fabric
rubber bands or string
apron
rubber gloves

1 Put on apron.
2 **Adult:** mix vegetable dyes or cold-water fabric dyes in separate
   containers according to the manufacturer's instructions.
3 Bunch or roll the fabric and bind it tightly at intervals with rubber
   bands or string, wrapping over the same spot several times.
4 Put on rubber gloves. Submerge the tied fabric in one dye bucket for a few
   minutes. Remove fabric and allow excess dye to drip off. Leave fabric until
   it is semi-dry then remove string and bands. Hang to dry thoroughly.
5 Repeat steps 4 and 5 with the second and third dyes.

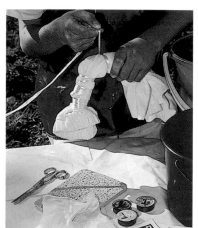

Bind fabric tightly and wind string or rubber bands over same spot several times.

Submerge bound fabric in dye bucket for a few minutes then allow excess dye to drip off.

reverse tie-dyeing

OVER
6
YEARS

you will need
liquid bleach
bucket or ice-cream container
cotton fabric or garment in dark
  colour (black, dark blue and
  blue denim work well)
string or rubber bands
apron
rubber gloves

1 **Adult:** pour bleach into bucket or ice-cream container.
2 Fold, twist, crumple or roll fabric or garment then bind tightly with
   string or rubber bands wrapping over the same spot several times.
3 Put on apron and rubber gloves. Dip the fabric or garment into
   bleach until the colour of the fabric changes, then allow excess
   bleach to drip off.
4 Rinse fabric or garment thoroughly in cold water until the water is
   no longer coloured. Remove the bands or string. Hang to dry.

Safety first
Ensure that bleach does not come in contact with skin. Keep lid on
bleach and keep it out of reach of children at all times.

*Bind fabric tightly and wind string or rubber
bands over same spot several times.*

*Submerge bound fabric in bleach for a few
minutes until the colour of the fabric changes.*

paper dyeing

you will need

various papers, such as rice paper sheets, coffee filter papers, blotting
   papers or paper towels (absorbent paper will give the best results)
food colourings mixed with water, in several bowls
eye droppers
apron

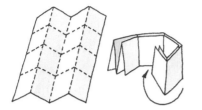

*Unusual folds make more interesting pictures.
Experiment with folds to see the effects.*

1 Put on apron.
2 Fold the sheets of paper into eighths or sixteenths.
3 Dip a corner of folded paper into a colour then remove.
4 Dip another corner into a second colour then remove.
5 Repeat with all corners of folded paper. Unfold and dry.

For variation, use eye droppers to create a colourful design
on the paper (in this case, there's no need to fold the paper).

Dip a corner of folded paper into one colour.

Then dip another corner into a second colour.

Repeat with all corners, using many colours.

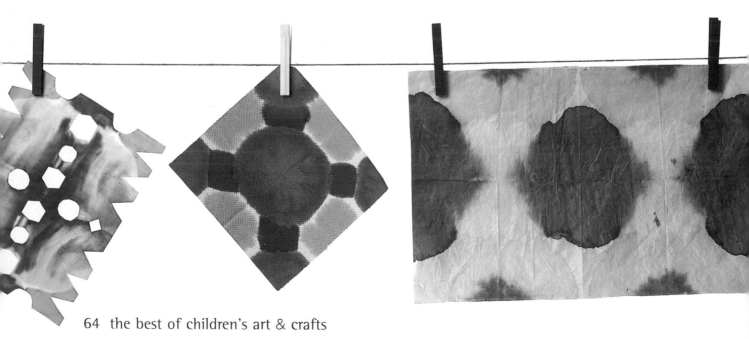

Fill eye dropper with colour from one bowl and drop spots of colour onto the paper.

Use another eye dropper to add a second colour and allow the colours to blend.

collage & construction

Collage is an exciting technique of pasting, gluing, taping and stapling materials such as paper, fabrics, dried foods, feathers, nuts and other objects. Encourage tactile exploration and use of objects to create `feeling´ pictures. Construction encourages children to further explore tactile and colour combinations. Working in three dimensions challenges children's imaginations and can present fascinating results. Allow children to work with a wide range of materials including recycled objects, which will enrich both collages and constructions.

paper collage

you will need
coloured paper or tissue paper
glue in tubs
brushes
paper or plastic sheet or lid

1 Tear coloured paper or tissue
   paper into different sized pieces.
2 Brush a coloured paper piece
   with glue then stick the paper
   piece onto the paper, plastic
   sheet or lid. Repeat to make a
   picture. Younger children
   often prefer to add glue directly
   to the paper or plastic then
   place the paper pieces onto it.
   Older children can arrange
   their collage materials into
   pictures; younger children
   will simply enjoy gluing
   materials onto the sheet.
   For see-through pictures, tissue
   paper gives the best result;
   the paper pieces overlap,
   causing colours to mix and
   blend. Tape see-through pictures
   to a window for display.

box sculpture

you will need

cardboard boxes, all shapes
  and sizes
cardboard cylinders
powder tempera
  paint (see page 6)
shallow bowl
paintbrush
collage materials
masking tape
heavy wool or string
PVA glue

1 Tape boxes and cylinders together to make space-age cities, trains, animals or abstract sculptures.
2 Make up powder tempera paint in shallow bowl. Paint cardboard sculpture. Glue on any collage materials.
3 String sculpture together with wool or string. Several small structures can be joined together.

note   If the sculpture is painted with a clear gloss enamel, the writing on the boxes will show through the paint.

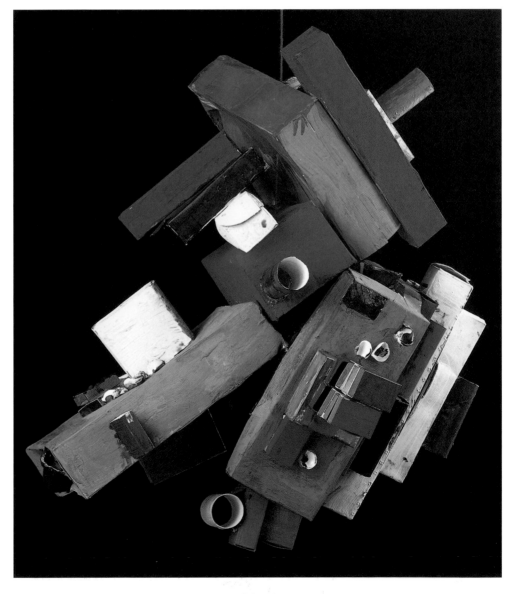

ALL
AGES

box car

Paint and decorate top and sides of upturned box in as many or as few colours as desired.

Using the paper fasteners, attach the metal pie plate headlights to the front of the box.

you will need

large cardboard box, top flaps cut off
powder paint in bowls
paintbrushes
4 large paper plates
paper fasteners, about
　2cm (¾in) in length
2 foil pie plates or small paper plates
　covered in foil
felt-tipped pen
small polystyrene packing tray
heavy string or cord
masking tape
stapler
scissors

1　**Adult:** using scissors, cut a hole in bottom of box large enough to slip over child's hips.

2　Turn box upside down. Paint top and sides of box. Allow to dry.

3　**Adult:** using scissors, pierce two holes in each long side of box, where wheels are to be attached. Pierce holes in centre of paper plates. Attach plates to sides of box with paper fasteners. Cover pointed ends of fasteners inside box with tape.

4　Use two foil pie plates as headlights. **Adult:** using scissors, pierce two holes in one short side of box, where headlights are to be attached. Pierce holes in centre of foil plates. Attach plates to box with paper fasteners. Cover pointed ends of fasteners inside box with tape.

5　Using felt-tipped pen, write your name on packing tray to make personalised number plate. Tape or staple to back of box.

6　**Adult:** using scissors, pierce hole in centre of each long side of box, at the top. Thread string or cord through one hole. Tie a double knot so it cannot slip through hole.

7　Step into box and pull it up to the waist. **Adult:** pull string or cord around back of child's neck, then thread through second hole. Tie a double knot to secure string or cord. The car is now ready for a ride.

Make a train by adding more boxes as carriages. Turn boxes upside-down on the ground, one behind the other, and children can climb aboard for a train ride.

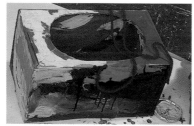

Make a number plate by writing your name on a polystyrene tray, then attach tray to box.

Tie rope to one side of box, place box over child, then adjust length of rope and tie to second side.

pea mobile

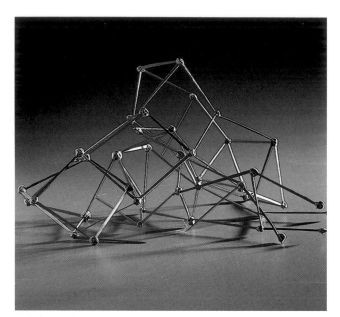

you will need
fresh pea pods
coloured toothpicks, preferably pointed
  at both ends (see how to dye, page 6)
string

1 Shell peas.
2 Stick toothpick into pea. Place pea on the other end of toothpick and stick another toothpick into same pea. Continue this process to create a geometric structure. Take care that no more than four toothpicks are stuck into each pea because the pea will fall apart.
3 When finished, allow peas to dry out for several days. Do not touch them while they're drying.
4 Tie string to structure and hang mobile from ceiling.

ALL AGES

chenille stick creatures

you will need
variety of chenille sticks,
  various colours, with short
  or shaggy fur

1 Twist chenille sticks into interesting animals and people. Odds and ends can be used for eyes and clothes. Let your imagination loose!

plastic cup flowers

you will need
coloured plastic cups
tissue paper or paper serviettes
stickers for decoration
drinking straws with
  bendable joint
vase, pot or branch
glue
adhesive tape
scissors

Cut the rim off a plastic cup, then fringe cup by cutting cup from rim almost to the base.

Trim a bendable drinking straw to desired size and tape to back of cup for a stem.

1 Using scissors, cut the rim off a plastic cup. Fringe the cup from the rim almost to the base, without breaking off the pieces. One cup can be glued inside another to make extra petals, if desired.

2 Gently bend the petals back. Crumple a piece of tissue paper or paper serviette and glue it into the base of the cup. Crumple tiny balls of a contrasting colour paper and glue them around the edge of the first paper centre. Decorate the flower with stickers.

3 Trim a drinking straw to desired size, tape to back of flower for the stem.

4 Arrange flowers in a vase or pot, or tape to a branch for display.

For variation, cut individual petal shapes from plastic cup or plate and glue together at the flower centre. Use the base of a second cup for the centre and fill with coloured cotton wool, or decorate with stickers.

windsock

Cut out the windsock through both layers of fabric, following the shape you have drawn.

Decorate the outside of the windsock with brightly coloured fabric scraps, sequins or braid.

With right sides together, stitch or staple the side seams, leaving top and bottom ends open.

Stitch a hoop around the mouth of the windsock then attach a cord at three places.

you will need

4 metres (about 4 yards) of
  lightweight fabric
fabric pencil or pen
fabric scraps in bright colours
sequins, braid, if desired
paper streamers
plastic, cane or wire hoop
4 metres (about 4 yards) strong cord
broom handle or thick dowel
PVA or fabric glue
needle and thread or sewing machine
stapler
scissors

1 Fold the fabric in half across the width to give a 2 metre (6½ft) length. Draw the windsock shape onto the fabric. A shape that will make a wind tunnel, opening at both ends, is needed. A fish works well.

2 Cut out the windsock shape through both layers of the fabric.

3 Decorate the outside of the windsock with fabric scraps, sequins or braid. We cut scallops and spots from fabric scraps and glued them to the main fabric.

4 With right sides together, stitch or staple the side seams of the windsock, leaving both top and bottom ends unstitched. Turn through to right side. Staple paper streamers to the bottom edge of the windsock.

5 Securely stitch a hoop around the mouth of the windsock. If the hoop is too large, cut a piece out and rejoin the hoop with tape. Attach the cord at three places around the hoop and onto the broom handle or dowel.

To fly the windsock attach it to a post outdoors or play with it like a hand-held kite.

battleship

you will need

2 x 1 litre (1¾ pint) milk cartons

foil

coloured cardboard cylinder

pen

cotton wool

chenille sticks

adhesive tape

scissors

1 Seal the open end of a milk carton with tape. Cut a piece of foil to fit around entire carton. Carefully cover milk carton with foil lengthways, so that the edges are on the underside of the boat. Tape the edges together.

2 **Adult:** cut off the bottom of the second milk carton about 6cm (2½in) from the base (the ship's upper deck). Turn the carton upside down, and place the cardboard cylinder (about 8cm [3in] high) in the middle of the base. The cylinder is the ship's funnel. Draw around the base of the cylinder with a pen. Pierce inside the circle and cut out a hole. Wrap the carton in foil, carefully folding the foil into the hole. Insert the cylinder into the hole. Decorate chimney with cotton wool for smoke.

3 Tape the chimney and top deck to the ship's body.

4 **Adult:** pierce the top of the ship's body with scissors and insert chenille sticks for aerials. Wrap a chenille stick around the bottom of the chimney.

Polystyrene blocks also make great ships. Decorate as desired.

raft

you will need
17 iceblock sticks
PVA glue
chenille stick
toothpicks

1 Arrange 12 iceblock sticks, side by side, so that they are close together. Leave a small gap between the last two sticks for the steering wheel. Apply glue to two more sticks and place the sticks, glue-side down, across both ends of the raft. Allow to dry.
2 Turn the raft over. Cut off the end (about 1cm [3/8in]) of a stick so that the edge is flat. Place the stick, upright, in the gap between the last two sticks. Apply glue to two more sticks and place the sticks, glue-side down, so that they are in the same place as the two sticks on the bottom of the raft. Allow raft to dry.
3 Bend a chenille stick into a circle and glue onto steering column with the chenille stick ends on the column. Glue toothpicks onto steering wheel for spokes.

cruise liner

you will need
1 litre (1³/₄ pint)
   milk carton
foil
cardboard cylinder
paper ring reinforcements
adhesive tape
scissors

1 Seal the open end of a milk carton with tape. Cut a piece of foil to fit around the entire carton. Carefully cover the milk carton with foil lengthways, so that the edges are on the underside of the boat. Tape the foil edges together.
2 Decorate liner with cardboard cylinders for funnels, and paper ring reinforcements for portholes.

vegetable sculpture

you will need
coloured toothpicks (see how to
    dye, page 6)
apples, oranges and various fruits
carrots, potatoes and various
    vegetables
sultanas,
    marshmallows,
    soft sweets,
    chenille sticks,
    to decorate

1 Using the toothpicks, stick a selection of fruits and vegetables together
    to form a sculpture or a creature. Choose foods that will be easy to stick
    toothpicks into; avoid hard foods. Vegetables could be cooked slightly so
    they are more easily pierced by the toothpicks. Decorate as desired.

salad clown

Children may be encouraged
to eat healthy foods if they are
presented in a fun way.

you will need
dinner plate (with a slight bowl works best)
mashed potato
lettuce leaves
hard-boiled egg slices
olive slices
chives
alfalfa
tomato
capsicum skin strip
carrot pieces
cucumber slices
knife

1 With a knife, spread mashed potato inside
    bowl of plate until smooth and flat.

2 Decorate clown with lettuce for hair, egg
    and olive slices for eyes, chives for eyelashes,
    alfalfa for eyebrows, end pieces of tomato
    for cheeks and nose, capsicum for mouth,
    cucumber slices for ears and carrot slices for
    bow tie. Let your imagination run wild!

78 the best of children's art & crafts

paper bag kite

you will need
large paper bag
paper ring reinforcements
string (2.4 metres or about 2½ yards)
paint in small bowls
paintbrushes
paper collage materials
tissue paper and crepe paper
   streamers
hole puncher
PVA glue
scissors

1 Punch hole on each of the four corners of the paper bag (at least 3cm [1¼in] from edge of bag). Put a paper ring reinforcement on each hole.
2 Cut two pieces of string to a length of about 80cm (about 2½ft). Tie each end of the string into an opposite hole to form two loops.
3 Cut a piece of string about 80cm (about 2½ft) long. Put it through the two loops and tie it. The string will act as a handle.
4 Paint paper bag kite as desired. Allow to dry.
5 Glue on paper collage materials and streamers. Allow to dry.
6 Open the paper bag kite. Hold onto the string and run so that the wind catches in the paper bag kite and makes it fly.

note Younger children will need help with steps 1, 2, 3.

collage kite

you will need
favourite painting or print
light-weight collage materials
string decorated with collage materials (for tail)
string
PVA glue
scissors

1 Cut a kite shape from an old painting or print.
2 Glue on any light-weight collage materials.
3 Tie on a tail made from any stringing materials. Tie a string on other end of kite. Hold on to string and run.

fish kite

you will need

foil liner from orange juice or
    wine cask
small plastic plate
coloured plastic shopping bag
2 plastic cups
paper fasteners or paper clips
felt-tipped pen
string
stapler
adhesive tape
hole puncher
scissors

Staple the plastic plate rim around the foil liner opening, at the mouth end of the fish.

Staple the intact end of the plastic bag fringe to the tail end of the fish's body.

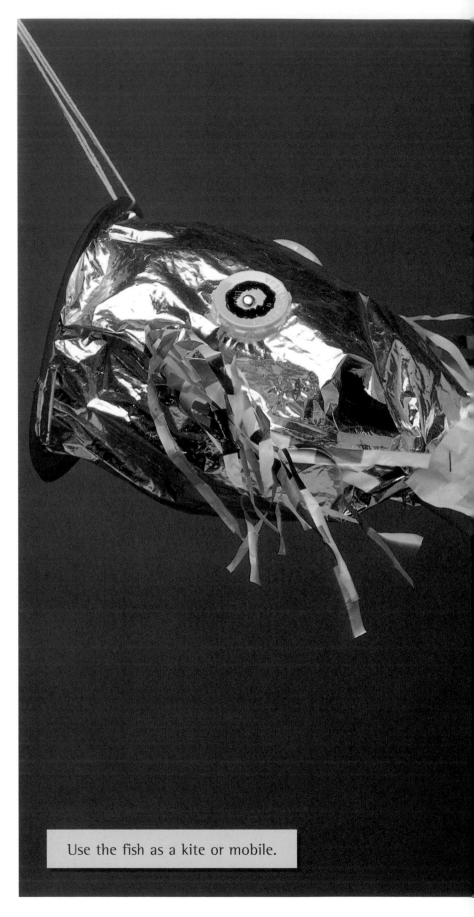

Use the fish as a kite or mobile.

1 **Adult:** cut the ends off the foil liner. Wash out the liner and remove plastic tap. This will be the body of the fish kite. Carefully cut out the centre of the plate leaving the rim intact. Staple the plate rim around the liner opening, at the mouth end. The plate will form the mouth.

2 Fold two or three tucks into the tail end of the liner. Cut the plastic bag into a fringe, leaving the strips of the fringe attached at one end. Staple a large piece of the fringe to the tail end, reserving some fringe for the fins.

3 Staple reserved fringe to fish body.

4 Cut the round base from two plastic cups for eyes (or use the remains of the plastic plate). Pierce a hole in the centre of each cup base with scissors and attach eyes to fish using paper fasteners. Draw details with felt-tipped pen.

5 **Adult:** punch a hole through the top of the mouth and thread the string through. Fly the kite.

Tape small pieces of plastic bag fringe to the sides of fish's body for fins.

Decorate the fish's plastic-cup eyes with a black felt-tipped pen.

collage & construction 81

multi-coloured glasses

you will need
egg carton
cellophane pieces
PVA glue or adhesive tape
scissors

1 **Adult:** using scissors make a
   large hole in each cup section
   of the carton.
2 Glue or tape pieces of coloured
   cellophane over each hole. Look
   through the cellophane glasses
   to see a colourful world.

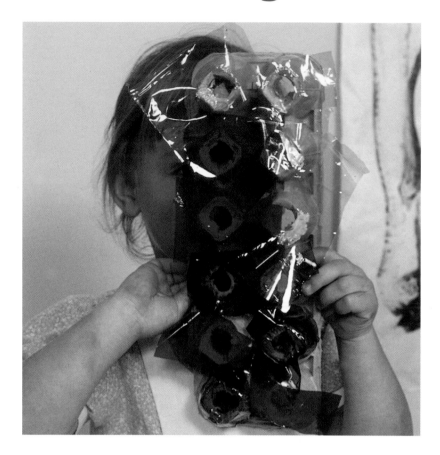

opera glasses

you will need
foil meal tray
cellophane pieces
iceblock stick
adhesive tape
scissors

1 **Adult:** using scissors, trim
   around a foil meal tray and cut
   two holes for the lenses.
2 Tape cellophane pieces over
   each hole. Tape an iceblock
   stick in the centre or at the side
   of the glasses, as desired.

binoculars

you will need
cellophane pieces
2 toilet roll cylinders
adhesive tape
string

1 Tape pieces of cellophane over the end
  of the two cylinders. Different coloured
  cellophane can be used for each one.
2 Tape the two cylinders together.
3 **Adult:** pierce a hole on the outside of
  each cylinder. Attach a string.

telescope

you will need
cellophane scrap
long cardboard cylinder
adhesive tape

1 Tape a piece of cellophane over one end of the cylinder.

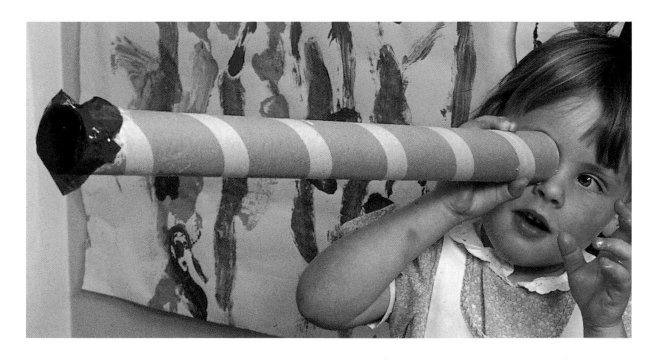

OVER 4 YEARS

box dragon

you will need

1 litre (1¾ pint) milk cartons
    (at least 8)
white and coloured paper
collage materials
egg carton cups or seashells
chenille sticks
beads, bottle caps or macaroni
wool
adhesive tape
PVA glue
paper fasteners or paper clips
scissors

1 **Adult:** pull top of milk carton fully open. From top, cut away the two creased sides, which are opposite each other. Repeat for each carton.

2 Cover outside of carton with white or coloured paper and tape into place. Glue collage materials onto cartons (or paint cartons).

3 **Adult:** to make dragon's head, cut off all of the top folded section of a carton. Starting at one top corner, cut a deep V into a side of the carton to about two-thirds of the way down, coming back up to the next top corner of the carton. Cut similarly on the opposite side of the carton. These are the dragon's jaws. Cover with paper and decorate with collage materials. Glue the egg carton cups or seashells onto the head for eyes.

4 **Adult:** to connect parts of the dragon, overlap top flaps of a carton onto the bottom of another milk carton. In the centre of this overlap, pierce two holes through both thicknesses of cartons with scissors. Push each end of a 10cm (4in) piece of chenille stick through each hole to inside of carton. Reach inside carton and twist together two ends of chenille sticks. Repeat with other side of the two cartons to connect them. Alternatively, paper fasteners or paper clips may be used instead of chenille sticks. Thread together beads, bottle caps or macaroni with wool to make a tail.

pegs

you will need
wooden spring clothes pegs
paint in small bowl
paintbrush
felt-tipped pens
cotton wool, fabric scraps,
　crepe paper or wool
PVA glue

1 Paint peg any colour.
2 Draw on features with felt-tipped pens.
3 Glue pieces of cotton wool, fabric, crepe
　paper or wool to make a creature or person.
　There is no end of possibilities when making
　peg creatures: crocodiles, lions, Santa Claus,
　buildings, birds and clowns are just a few ideas.

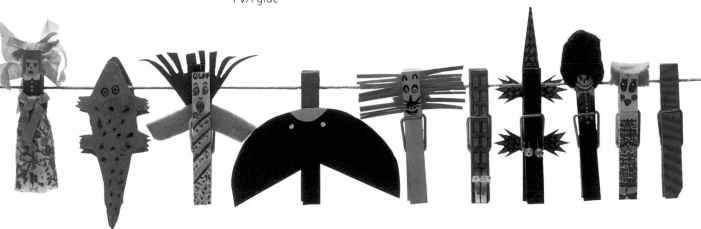

rock painting

you will need
powder paint in small bowls
paintbrushes
smooth rocks
chenille sticks
clear gloss enamel or spray varnish
PVA glue

1 Paint any abstract or animal
　design onto rock (eg cat, mouse,
　fish, owl, flower, human face or
　beetle). Allow to dry thoroughly.
2 If desired, glue on chenille
　sticks for tails, feelers or legs.
3 **Adult:** paint rock with clear
　gloss enamel or spray varnish.

skittles

you will need

newspaper

funnel

several empty plastic bottles

clean sand

paper paste or

   cornflour paste (see page 8)

paint in small bowls

paintbrushes

PVA glue

wool and other collage materials

clear gloss enamel

1 Crumple double sheets of newspaper into roughly round shapes for the heads, pulling out longish pieces for the necks.

2 Using a funnel, fill each plastic bottle about one-third full of sand. The sand helps prevent bottles from falling over too easily.

3 Push the newspaper necks and heads into the mouths of the bottles, ensuring there is a tight fit. Tear remaining newspaper into largish strips; dip strips into paper paste or cornflour paste so that they are covered all over with paste. Stick newspaper strips all over the heads and down onto the necks, to secure newspaper heads to bottles. Continue sticking newspaper strips to bottles until they are completely covered with two or three layers of newspaper. Allow bottles to dry for a few days.

4 Paint the heads of the bottles and allow to dry. Paint the bodies of the bottles in colourful designs; allow to dry.

5 Paint eyes, noses and mouths on heads; allow to dry. Glue wool on for hair and decorate bodies with collage materials; allow to set.

6 **Adult:** paint the bottles with clear gloss enamel; allow to dry.

Stand skittles up and try to knock them all over with a ball.

tip A fast and easy alternative is to papier-mâché the heads and necks only, then attach to bottles using strong tape. Apply paint and other decorations directly to the plastic bottles and the papier-mâché heads.

box puzzle

you will need
child's drawing or painting
ruler
felt-tipped pen
empty matchboxes
PVA glue
scissors

1 Select a favourite drawing or painting, preferably one that is simple but solidly coloured.

2 **Adult:** using the ruler and the felt-tipped pen, mark off the matchboxes on the back of the drawing, making marks across the top and down the sides of the paper. Draw vertical and horizontal lines on the paper to join the marks and create matchbox shapes.

3 Using scissors, follow the lines and cut out the rectangles. Glue each piece of the drawing, right-side up, to the top of each matchbox. Arrange the boxes to match the original drawing.

collage & construction 87

pressed flowers

you will need
fresh flowers
newspapers
heavy books

1 Gather fresh flowers on a nature walk.
2 Lay them out individually on a newspaper so they are not touching. Put several sheets of newspaper on top of them. Put books or any flat, heavy weight on top of the newspaper. Leave them about four weeks to dry out thoroughly. Thick flowers take longer.

note Pressed dried flower arrangements are delicate and should be handled with care.

> Leaf skeletons make delicate and pretty patterns.

wall pictures

you will need
wooden curtain rings
sheet of heavy paper
pen
saucer
small pressed flowers
scribble paper
toothpicks
PVA glue
scissors

1 Place curtain ring on heavy paper. Draw around outside of ring, keeping pen close to ring. Cut out circle about ½cm (¼in) on the inside of the drawn circle.
2 Put a few drops of glue into saucer. Put paper circle on table with pressed flowers spread out near it. Choose one flower and place it upside down on scribble paper. Dip thicker end of toothpick into glue and apply lightly to back of flower.
3 Carefully lift flower and place it glue-side down on paper circle. Repeat this process until design is complete.
4 Put curtain ring on table. Apply one circle of glue to back of ring (a squeeze bottle is easiest). Lift up ring and place it glue-side down on top of flower arrangement (with the screw eye at top of arrangement). The ring becomes a frame for the arrangement and the screw eye can hang on a hook.

plaster hands

you will need

casting plaster (available from hardware stores)
2 large ice-cream containers
powder paint
water
spoon
large paper clip
paper or plastic plate

1 Pour plaster powder into an ice-cream container (use about 500 grams (about 1lb) per hand). Make up two to three hands worth of plaster at a time.
2 Add paint powder. Add enough water to the plaster so the consistency seems rough and cracked but is smooth when a spoon is run over the top. Stir plaster thoroughly.
3 Bend open paper clip a little as illustrated and place near top of plate. Scoop plaster into plate, press down and smooth over.
4 Plaster is ready when it holds the shape of a finger when pressed into it. Plaster is usually ready as soon as it is put in the plate. Press hand into plaster and remove hand quickly.
5 Leave plaster overnight to harden. Remove from plate. Dig around paper clip a little and use it to hang on a nail in the wall.

Bend open the paper clip a little and place it near the top of the plate.

Press your hand into the plaster, and quickly but carefully remove it.

nature garden

you will need

play dough (see page 9) or casting plaster (available from hardware stores)
heavy paper plate
leaves, flowers, seed pods, twigs, rocks, weeds and so on (these can be collected on a nature walk)

1 Spread play dough or made-up casting plaster into bottom of paper plate.
2 Press leaves, flowers and other objects into play dough or plaster to make a nature garden.

Press nature objects into the play dough base.

paper hangings

you will need

sheet of graph paper

string

sheets of coloured paper (for
    animal features)

a sheet of cardboard (for spatter
    painting stencil)

toothbrush

powder paint mixed
    in small bowls

comb or wire screen

felt-tipped pen

PVA glue

stapler

scissors

1 To make fluted circles, concertina or fan–fold along heavy lines on rectangular graph paper (ours measured 72cm [28in] x 36 cm [14in]).

2 Tie string at centre of folded paper and glue either side to make a circle.

3 Animal features such as ears or a nose can be cut out of pieces of coloured paper, then folded, and stapled to the circle.

4 If spatter painting, cut cardboard stencils for shapes or features such as eyes and mouth. Place cut out stencils on circle and spatter paint by moving a toothbrush dipped in paint across a comb or wire screen.

5 Draw details of animal features onto circle with a felt-tipped pen.

6 Staple string to hang on wall or tape an ice block stick to circle to make a fan.

note Younger children may need help with steps 1, 2 and 6.

Concertina or fan-fold rectangular paper.

Cut out stencils and spatter paint the paper.

string collage

ALL AGES

you will need
colourful string or wool
paper paste or liquid starch (see
    page 8)
polystyrene tray
sheet of heavy paper
scissors

1 Cut string or wool into
    30cm (12in) lengths. Soak
    for a few minutes in polystyrene
    tray of paste or starch.
2 Place tray along top edge of
    paper. Pull one paste-covered
    strand out of the tray and
    arrange it on paper into desired
    design. Repeat with different
    coloured string or wool.

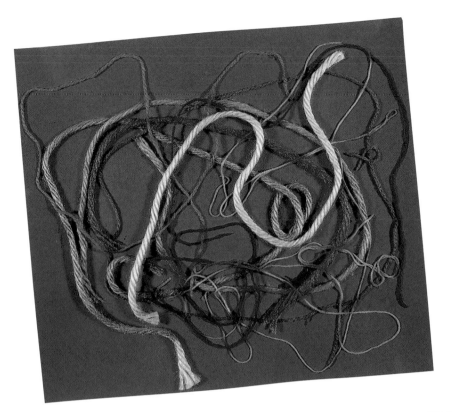

paper dolls

OVER 4 YEARS

you will need
doll shapes drawn onto
    heavy paper
crayons
wool, fabric scraps, buttons
PVA glue
scissors

1 Cut out various doll shapes.
2 Colour dolls with crayons. Older
    children may draw faces on dolls.
3 Glue wool, fabric scraps and
    buttons onto doll to dress it.

neighbourhood collage

you will need
sheets of coloured paper
large sheet of paper
felt-tipped pens
glue
scissors

1 Ask children to draw their family home, garden, pets, cars and family friends on coloured paper.
2 **Adult:** cut out pictures.
3 Glue pictures onto sheet of paper.

A neighbourhood collage is a great project for a group of children. Each child can add the elements that are important in his or her neighbourhood. It's a stimulating way for children to show how they see their own environment.

abstract collage

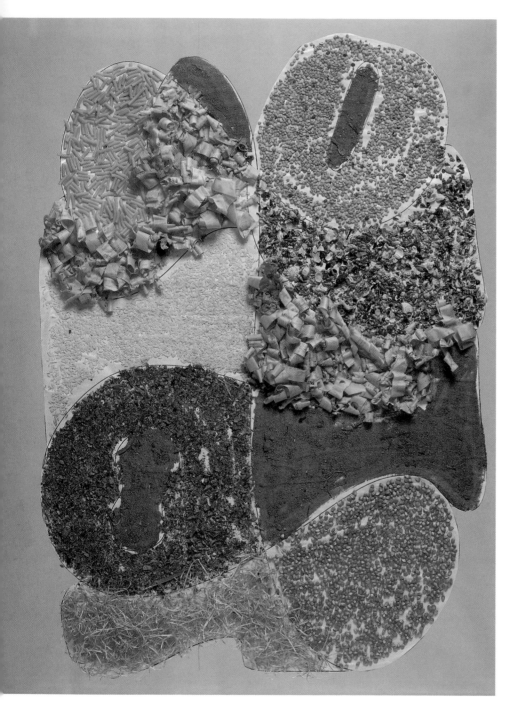

you will need
sheet of heavy paper or paper
   plates or cardboard boxes
macaroni, spaghetti, beans,
   seeds, cereals, sand, shells
PVA glue

1 Cover small area of paper or
  item to be decorated with glue.
2 Stick on macaroni, spaghetti,
  beans, seeds and cereals.
3 Repeat steps 1 and 2 until
  remainder of item is covered
  with the collage materials.

For variation, draw a design
on paper and fill the design
with different collage materials.

wood collage

you will need
cardboard
wood scraps, all shapes
    and sizes
wood shavings
coloured paper scraps
pencil
PVA glue
scissors

1 Draw an animal, person or
   your house onto cardboard
   (we drew a teddy bear).
   Adult: cut out the shape.
2 Glue a variety of wood scraps
   and shavings onto the shape.
   Leave collage to dry.
3 Cut out features for your
   wood collage from coloured
   paper scraps (we gave our
   bear eyes, nose and a mouth).
   Glue features onto collage.

papier-mâché animals

you will need

balloons (blown up and tied
  with a double knot)

foil

cardboard

cardboard cylinders, all sizes

newspaper

paper paste (see page 8)

clean sand

white powder tempera paint or
  sheet of white paper

powder paint in small bowls

large and small paintbrushes

clear gloss enamel, if desired

masking tape

scissors

1 Construct a general animal shape or fantasy creature by taping together balloons, wads of foil, cardboard and cardboard cylinders.

2 Tear newspaper into strips about 5cm (2in) x 15cm (6in). Dip strips into paper paste and stick onto animal shape. Cover animal shape with about four layers of newspaper. Allow to dry for several days.

3 If the animal doesn't sit up, cut a small hole in the bottom with scissors and puncture the balloon. Put about one cup of sand into the animal. Cover the hole with five or six layers of masking tape. The sand will make the animal sit upright.

4 Cover animal with white powder tempera paint and allow to dry. The paint will prevent newsprint from showing through when the shape is glossed. Alternatively, the shape may be covered with white paper and paste, instead of paint.

5 Paint animal with main colour and allow to dry thoroughly. This will prevent the colours from each coat mixing. Paint on other colours and allow to dry. Using a small brush, paint on details, such as eyes and nose. Allow to dry thoroughly.

6 **Adult:** for a finished look, paint animal with clear gloss enamel.

Create a whole menagerie of papier-mâché animals and fanciful creatures.

bangles

you will need
cardboard
newspaper
paper paste
white powder tempera paint or
   sheet of white paper
powder paint in small bowls
felt-tipped pens
liquid starch
coloured tissue paper
clear gloss enamel, if desired
stapler
scissors

1 **Adult:** cut a cardboard strip about 28cm (11in) long and as wide as a bangle, about 2cm (¾in) to 4cm (1½in). Overlap the ends until the strip fits over the child's hand loosely, allow for thickness added by papier-mâché. Staple together the ends of the cardboard strip.

2 Tear newspaper into small strips about 2cm (¾in) x 6cm (2½ in). Dip a piece of newspaper into paper paste and wrap newspaper around the bangle. Repeat this process until the bangle has been covered all over with at least three layers of newspaper.

3 Cover the bangle with thin white paper; or if painting with white paint allow bangle to dry completely otherwise the newspaper will show through, especially if the bangle is glossed. It may take several days for the papier-mâché to dry. (Bangles may be placed in microwave on defrost cycle for 5-10 minutes to speed up drying).

4 Decorate bangles by painting or drawing on them or covering them with liquid starch and layers of coloured tissue paper.

5 **Adult:** when dry, paint with clear gloss enamel.

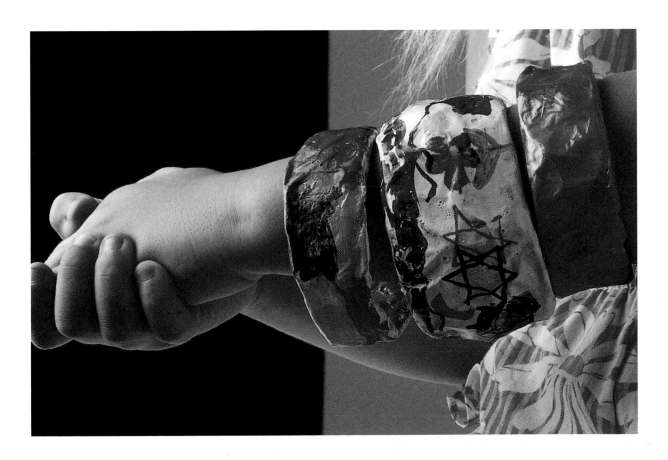

weaving &
stitching

Fibres, yarns and fabrics provide new tactile
experiences, and weaving and sewing help
develop the fine motor skills of small
hands as well as hand-eye co-ordination.
Try not to expect each child's work to exactly
replicate the pictures in this book. Treat our
projects as a starting point and encourage
children to develop their own ideas.

99

nature weaving

you will need

4 sticks about 20cm (8in) long
string
twigs, long grasses, fleece, weeds,
   feathers, flowers and other
   natural objects
scissors

1 Make a square frame by binding the four sticks together
   with string at each of the four corners.
2 Wind string firmly around one of the sticks and knot or wrap the
   end. Then wind the string onto the stick opposite. Continue winding
   string from end to end at regular intervals until the frame is full.
   Cut the string and tie end to the frame. These are the warp strings.
3 Starting from one end, weave twigs, grasses, feathers and
   other materials under and over the warp strings. Continue until
   strings are covered. This weaving makes a beautiful hanging.

Make a square frame by binding the four sticks together with string at each corner.

Wind string firmly around one of the sticks, knot the end, then wind it onto opposite stick.

Starting from one end, weave the natural materials under and over the strings.

This weaving gives children
an opportunity to explore the
characteristics of natural materials.

branch weaving

you will need

branch with at least three smaller
   branches shooting out from it
coloured wools, each about
   2 metres (2 yards) in length
long grasses, feathers, seashells,
   corn husks, seed pods and
   other natural objects

1 Starting at the top or bottom
of one small branch, loop wool
around a branch to secure it.
Continue to next small branch
and loop wool around it and
then to the next branch.
Continue to wrap wool around
smaller branches to make a
warp base moving up or down
branches, depending on where
weaving began. Warp threads
are the first threads on the
frame. They are stretched
lengthwise and usually placed
side by side on the frame.

2 Weave wool, grasses and other
intriguingly shaped items
through warp wool strands.
Some children may prefer
to wrap wool around branches
in a random manner.

woven wall hanging

you will need

coloured wool, about 2 metres
   (2 yards) in length
U-shaped branch
feathers, leaves, wild grasses,
   bamboo, leather strips

1 Tie wool at one end of branch and
stretch to opposite end. Tie off
wool in a knot. Leave about 3cm
(1¼in) between each length of
wool. Repeat stretching wool until
you have filled the available space.

2 Thread through, under and over,
materials such as feathers, leaves,
grasses, bamboo and leather strips.

OVER 8 YEARS

weaving on a box loom

you will need

iceblock sticks

cardboard box

fabric strips or wool

2 dowel rods (at least as wide as the cardboard box)

strip of cord

masking tape

scissors, if needed

1 Tape iceblock sticks, half-way down the stick, at regular intervals along one end of the box. At opposite end of box, tape sticks in line with the first row.

2 Tie a fabric strip or length of wool to the first stick at one end. Take the strip around the first stick at the opposite end, then back again to the next stick on the opposite end. Keep stretching the fabric strip taut. Continue until all sticks are looped. These first strips are the warp threads.

3 Beginning at one end of box, weave fabric strips or wool under and over the warp strips. Continue weaving until warp strips are covered.

4 When weaving is complete, carefully slip the weaving off the sticks and thread the dowel rods through the loops at each end of the weaving. Secure the loose ends by threading these back into the weaving.

5 Attach a hanging cord to the top dowel. Use as a wall hanging.

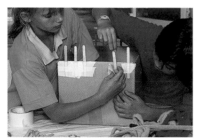

Tape iceblock sticks, half-way down the stick, at regular intervals along one end of the box.

The warp or first threads are stretched from one end of the box to the other.

The weft threads are woven over and under the warp threads to create the weaving.

Make several box weavings, then join them together to make a floor mat!

drinking straw weaving

you will need

6 x 1 metre (about 1 yard) lengths of yarn (or length desired)

6 drinking straws

yarns, various colours

scissors

1. Tie the six lengths of yarn together at one end to form a knot. Thread the untied ends of each yarn through a straw, push straws close to the knot.
2. Tie a loose knot at the other end of the straws to hold them in place.
3. Weave coloured yarn over and under the straws (which cover the warp threads). Join new yarn by tying it to the previous length. When you have woven about half the length of the straws, undo the knot at the bottom and slide the straws down a little, keeping the top of the straws inside the weaving at all times. Continue weaving until fabric is the desired length.
4. When the weaving is finished, remove the straws and tie the adjacent strings together. Trim then thread the string ends back into the weaving. Use the weaving as an unusual glitter strap or belt.

Substitute cardboard fabric rolls for straws and fabric strips for yarn.

Thread the untied ends of each yarn through a straw, push straws close to the knot.

Weave the coloured yarn over and under the straw-covered warp threads.

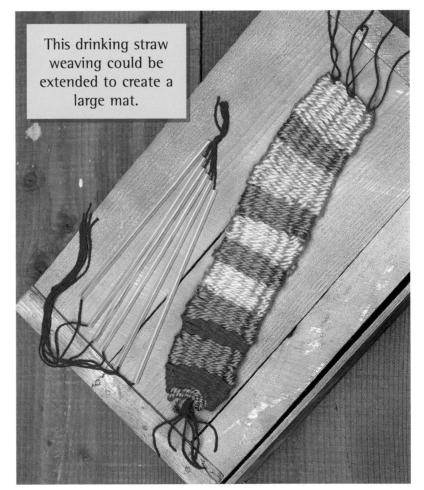

This drinking straw weaving could be extended to create a large mat.

appliquéd placemat

you will need

40cm (16in) x 30cm (12in)
  hessian fabric
felt
pins
wool or sewing thread
bodkin or large needle
buttons, braid or lace
scissors

1 Fringe the hessian fabric by removing the threads along each edge.
2 Cut out felt shapes to make a design. Pin felt pieces onto hessian.
3 Using sewing thread or wool and a bodkin or needle, stitch the felt pieces to the hessian (for tips on using needles, see page 5). First knot the thread then bring the needle up through the fabric from the wrong side. To finish each thread length, take the needle through to the back of the fabric and make two small secure stitches on top of each other. Embroidery stitches can be used (see diagrams at right).
4 Stitch buttons, braid or lace onto the placemat as desired.

Arrange the different felt pieces into design before stitching them onto the mat.

First knot the thread then bring the needle up through the fabric from the wrong side.

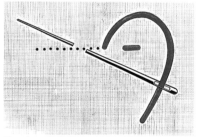

Running stitch

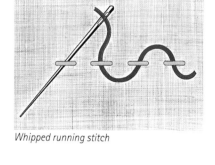

Whipped running stitch

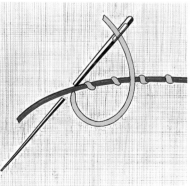

Couching

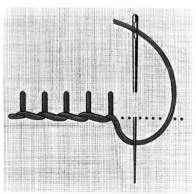

Blanket stitch

sewing cards
for beginners

you will need

child's drawing

cardboard

hole puncher

wool, threaded through a bodkin,
  if desired

buttons, macaroni, straws

glue

scissors

1 Glue child's drawing onto the cardboard. **Adult:** using
   scissors, cut the drawing into the desired shape.

2 **Adult:** punch holes along the edge of the drawing and
   as far into the centre as is possible.

3 Sew or thread wool through holes (for tips on using
   needles, see page 5). Buttons, macaroni, or cut straws
   may be added to wool while threading through holes.

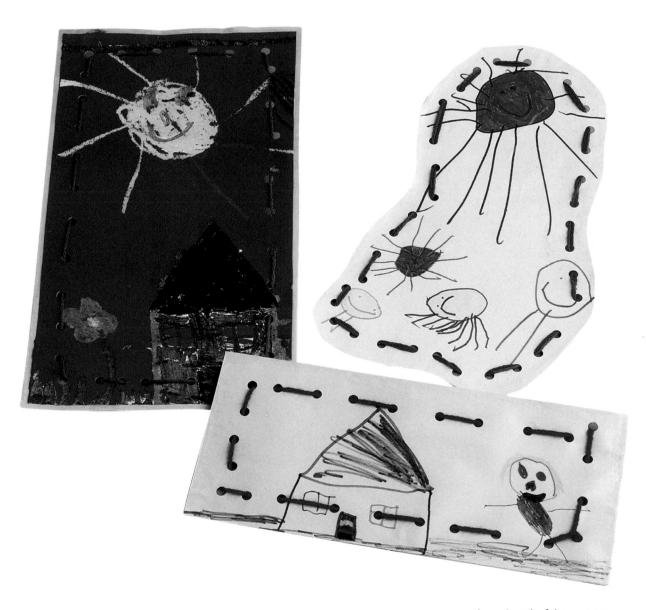

weaving trays

you will need

polystyrene packing trays

wool threaded through a
  darning needle (see page 5)

ribbon, wool, long reeds or grass
  for weaving

seashells or seed pods

knife

1 **Adult:** cut a geometric section in centre of the tray and remove it; a rectangle is easiest for a beginner to use.

2 Tie knot in end of threaded wool. Put threaded needle through tray, about 3cm (1¼in) in from edge of cut-out shape. Pull the wool across to other side and bring needle up through tray.

3 Repeat this process back and forth across cut-out section to make warp threads. Threads strung in one direction only (eg left to right) tend to make square or rectangular weaves whereas wool strung in all directions across cut-out shape enables unusual circles to be woven.

4 Weave ribbon or double thread of wool back and forth in a straight line or weave one or more circles depending on design of warp strings. To keep weaving square, push needle through side of tray after completing a line then continue weaving. Seashells or seed pods can be strung onto wool during weaving. Long reeds or grasses may also be used in place of ribbon or wool. Younger children need supervision until they have had a little practice. Trays can be used as placemats or wall hangings, or the ends of the warp strings can be cut from the tray, tied together two at a time (to stop weaving from coming undone), to be used as pot holders.

mesh stitching

you will need
orange or onion mesh bag
coloured cardboard
colourful yarn
masking tape
scissors

1 **Adult:** cut the bag to give a
  flat piece of mesh fabric. Trim the
  edges of the cardboard to make
  a frame. Cut a piece from the
  inside of the cardboard frame;
  it could be an irregular shape
  such as a heart or a simple star.

2 Tape mesh to the wrong
  side of the cardboard frame.
  Trim excess mesh.

3 Wrap a small piece of tape
  around the end of a yarn
  length (this makes the yarn
  end stiff enough to thread
  through the mesh). Using the
  coloured yarns, stitch patterns
  through the holes in the mesh.

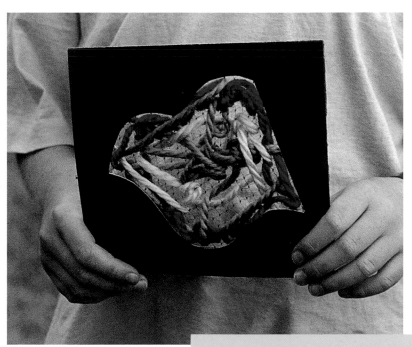

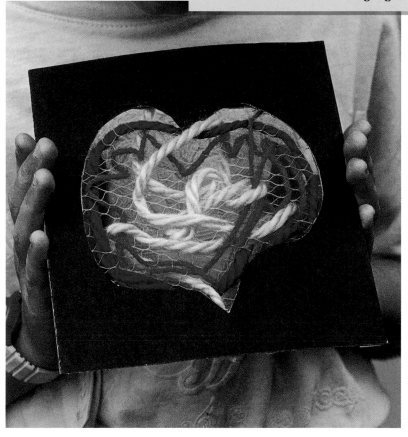

Mesh stitching makes an unusual
wall or window hanging.

Securely tape mesh to the cardboard frame.

Stitch patterns through the holes in the mesh.

necklaces & bracelets

you will need

wool, embroidery thread, elastic
thread or ribbon on bodkin
macaroni, seashells, seed pods,
buttons, beads

1 **Adult:** knot the first item to be threaded onto the end of the wool,
thread, or ribbon to prevent other items slipping off.

2 Thread items onto wool, thread or ribbon to make an interesting pattern.
Long necklaces can be joined in a knot. Bracelets must be threaded onto
elastic thread so they will stretch over a hand. Short necklaces can be
put on elastic thread, or a hook and eye can be used as a clasp. A necklace
may also be tied around the neck each time it is worn. First, tie a large
knot at each end of thread to stop items from slipping off.

Seashells and seed pods will need to have holes drilled into them to
enable them to be threaded onto the wool or thread (see project on right).

shell wind chime

OVER 4 YEARS

you will need
electric drill with steel bit
seashells
strong coloured wool
branch of driftwood
scissors

1 **Adult:** drill a hole in one end of each seashell.

2 Cut wool into lengths of about 1 metre (about 1 yard).

3 **Adult:** hang up the branch so that it is at child's working level.

4 Cut a length of wool at least 50cm (about 20in) long. Tie it to the branch. Thread a seashell onto the other end. Push shell close to the branch, tie a double knot to hold in place. Repeat with other shells, leaving space between. An adult may need to hold shells while the child ties them into place.

5 Thread and knot shells into other parts of branch. Take care not to make one side heavier than the other. Try to tie shells close enough to touch shells on other string when the wind blows. Wind chimes can also be made from hollow dried bamboo sections or from metal bottle tops.

ALL AGES

string balloon

you will need
thick, sturdy balloon
20 pieces of colourful wool or cotton string, about 60cm
  (24in) in length
extra strong homemade liquid starch (see page 8)

1 Blow up the balloon and tie a double knot in the end of it.
2 Dip a string in starch mixture, making sure it is completely covered
  with starch but not too heavy to hang on balloon. Wrap starched string
  around balloon, making sure both ends of string are securely plastered
  down. Repeat the process until the balloon is well covered with string
  but not completely covered so that string starts to slip off.
3 Allow balloon and string to dry overnight.
4 Pop balloon and remove it from string.

Coloured tissue paper can be added on top of the starched
wool or cotton to give a different effect.

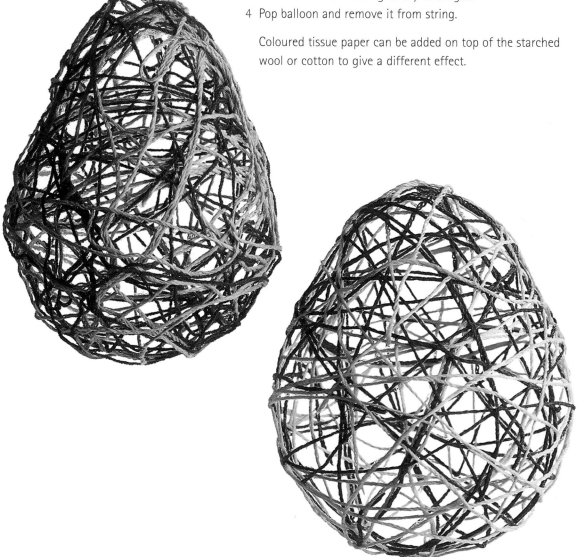

simple mobiles

you will need

wool lengths, about 70cm (28in)
straws, cut into 3cm
  (1¼in) lengths
macaroni, cotton reels,
  buttons, seashells,
paper shapes, cake patty pans
scissors

1 Starting 10cm (4in) into wool,
tie a knot around a large object
to make the top of the mobile.
2 Thread other interesting
objects onto wool alternating
with lengths of straw. The last
object should be threaded and
knotted with the wool.

tactile play

Sensory awareness goes hand in hand with
creativity. Projects in this chapter will stimulate
children's imaginations through exploration of
texture, temperature and colour, and will
arouse their curiosity. Many of these projects
are inexpensive, require little preparation
and are guaranteed to be fun!

coloured ice melts

you will need

plastic containers of various
   sizes and shapes, suitable for
   freezing, filled with water
food colouring
large plastic containers

1 **Adult with children:** in each of the plastic containers filled with water, add food colouring to water. Freeze the different containers overnight.
2 Look at the patterns formed in the ice by the food colouring; colour will either freeze evenly or coagulate in patches in the ice.
3 Empty coloured ice into a large container of water. Does the ice float or sink? Watch the ice melt; colours will mix, swirl and blend together in the water. Add more food colouring to see the effects. Add dark colours to the bowl last as they will eventually give a dark murky colour to the water.
4 Feel the shapes of the ice. How does the ice feel? Discuss why ice melts.

Do the iceblocks float or sink in the water?

Look at the patterns of colour in the ice.

slime

you will need

1 cup Lux soap flakes
2 litres (3½ pints) warm water
large plastic container
a pinch of food colouring
egg beaters
kitchen gadgets such as a funnel,
   cup, whisk, soup ladle, a
   scoop, soap drainers, punnets,
   sponges, jugs, etc

1 **Adult:** dissolve soap flakes in
warm water in a large
plastic container. Add food
colouring. Allow mixture to
stand until it becomes thick;
add more water if necessary.
2 **Adult:** beat mixture with egg
beaters. Children can help too!
3 Use the kitchen gadgets to pour,
measure, scoop, beat and whisk.
Children can also use words to
describe how the mixture feels
and what they are doing.

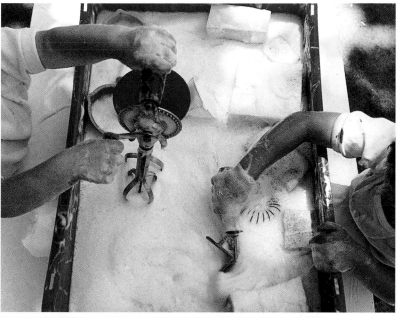

*Children enjoy slime but need careful
supervision to avoid soap getting in their eyes.*

tactile play 115

mix & mess

you will need

large containers of seeds, dried
  peas, beans, lentils, rice, grains,
  tea, cereal, etc
plastic containers for mixing
spoons, scoops, tongs,
  cup measures

1 **Adult:** arrange containers of
  seeds, etc in the centre of a
  table outdoors or on an easy-
  to-clean area. Give a container
  to each child for mixing.
2 Use scoops, spoons, tongs and
  cup to mix, measure, stir and
  pour, but don't eat!

*Gather lots of different seeds, dried peas,
beans, lentils, grains and cereals.*

*Use scoops, spoons, tongs and cups to mix,
measure, stir and pour the different foods.*

Children will enjoy the texture and consistency
of the ingredients and the fun of `cooking'.

floating & sinking

you will need

large container

food colouring

objects which will float or sink, for example, ping pong balls, golf balls, blocks, kitchen gadgets, sponges, strainers, straws, stones, flowers, corks, confetti, etc

1 **Adult:** working outdoors, fill the container with water. Add food the colouring to the water.

2 **Adult supervision:** child drops the objects into the water and observes floating and sinking. The child can guess which objects will sink and which will float. Talk about why this happens. Children will also enjoy pouring, and squeezing water from sponges and playing with the objects in the water.

Children can close their eyes and guess which objects they are touching in the water.

OVER 2 YEARS

goop

you will need
2 cups (16 fluid oz) water
food colouring
600g (1lb 3oz) cornflour
large container
apron

1 **Adult:** mix the water and food colouring into the cornflour in a large container. The goop should have a thick consistency; add extra water if necessary.
2 Put on apron. Plunge hands into the goop and feel the consistency. Use words to describe the feeling: `sticky´, `slimy´, `cool´, etc.
3 Enjoy exploring the behaviour of goop; it runs through the fingers, swirls slowly and has a pleasant, heavy feeling.

Mix water and colouring into the cornflour. It will take some time to mix it all together.

Encourage children to play with the goop before it is mixed. What does it feel like?

Goop should have a thick consistency. Run your fingers through it. What does it feel like?

This activity looks messy but clean-up is quite easy, goop can be picked up or wiped off the table and easily washed off hands. However, aprons should be worn.

leaf rubbings

you will need

leaves (not too small)
thin sheet of paper
adhesive tape
crayons

1 Place leaves on a table. Place the paper on top of the leaves. Tape the paper to the table to stop the paper from moving.

2 Remove paper label from crayon. Place crayon lengthways on paper and rub it back and forth across paper. The veins and ridges of the leaves will appear on the paper. Coins and other objects can also be rubbed in this way.

texture rubbings

you will need
textured objects such as fans,
bark, packaging plastic, combs,
braid, laces, fabric, coins
sheet of paper
crayons

1 **Adult:** flimsy materials such
as braid and lace can be glued,
pinned or taped onto a board
to keep them rigid.
2 Select a few textured objects.
Place paper over the textured
surfaces. Rub paper with crayon.
3 Try mixing crayon colours and
using several textured surfaces
on the one sheet of paper.

Older children might like to make
a texture rubbing as above but
use white candles instead of
crayons. Then paint over the paper
with a thin water-based paint.

*For this texture rubbing, we used a fan
which was woven out of cane.*

*Use white candles instead of crayons and
then paint over the paper with thin paint.*

beads to wear

you will need

¾ cup flour
½ cup cornflour
½ cup salt
vegetable dye or food colouring
bowl
90ml (3 fluid oz) warm water
toothpicks
clear gloss enamel

All play dough recipes may be used for jewellery, however those recipes made with salt tend to have a white residue which is particularly noticeable on dark-coloured play dough.

1 Mix first five ingredients in bowl. Add warm water gradually until mixture can be kneaded into a stiff dough. Dust with flour to reduce stickiness.

2 Mixture may be rolled into balls for beads. Pierce each bead with a toothpick then gently make circular movements to increase the size of the hole. Allow to dry for a few days. Large beads take longer to dry.

3 Holes should be checked after a day to see if they need punching. Paint if desired. This recipe makes a reasonably smooth dough that retains colour when dry. If desired, coat beads with clear gloss enamel to bring out colour.

Roll the dough into balls or other interesting shapes to make attractive beads.

Pierce the bead with a toothpick and gently make a circular movement to make a hole.

play dough creatures

you will need
different coloured play dough
  (see page 9)
plastic eyes or buttons
chenille sticks

1 Mould colourful dough into unusual creatures. Roll or pound play dough into fat round shapes, long thin sausage shapes or odd geometric shapes.
2 Add different coloured play dough or stick-on plastic eyes, buttons or chenille sticks to make interesting features. There's no end to the fantastic creations a child's imagination can produce from supple play dough.

clay wind chime

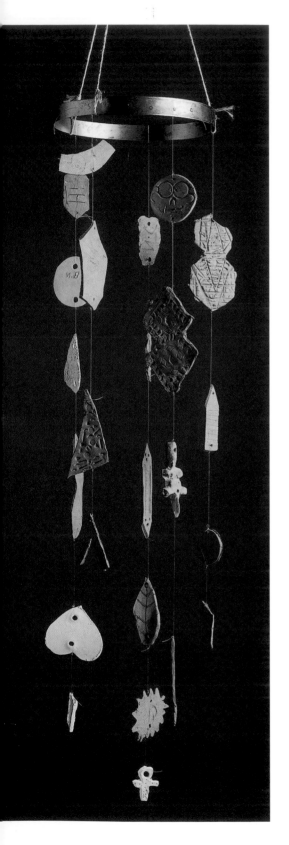

you will need

clay (see page 6)

tools such as nails, biscuit cutters,
   garlic press, knives

spatula

fishing line

coat-hanger or branch

rolling pin

ceramic kiln

1 **Adult:** knead a small portion of
clay to ensure that there are no
air bubbles in it. (Clay with air
bubbles in it will explode when it is
fired in a kiln.) Roll out the clay to
1cm (³⁄₈in) to 2cm (³⁄₄in) thick.

2 Cut desired shape out of flat clay.
Using the tools, gently press texture
marks into clay shape and attach
additional pieces of clay. Make a hole
in the top and bottom of each piece
for hanging. Slide spatula under
shape and move it to a place to
dry. Make a dozen or more different
shapes for wind chimes.

3 **Adult:** when thoroughly dry take the
shapes to a school or craft shop kiln
to be bisque fired. This gives them the
ringing quality of wind chimes.

4 **Adult:** tie short pieces of fishing
line through the holes in the chimes.
About four knots need to be made in
fishing line to keep items in place. Tie
three or four chimes together in a row
to make a string of chimes. Tie strings
of chimes to a branch or coat-hanger.
The fishing line gives the chimes a
better tone, but wool may be used.

paperweight

you will need
clay (see page 6)
paint (powder paint is suitable)
  mixed in small bowls
paintbrushes
clear gloss enamel or lacquer

1 Make the fish (right) or any
   shape desired out of the clay.
   Make patterns in the shape.
   Flatten the bottom of the shape
   and allow to dry overnight.
2 Paint designs onto the clay.
3 **Adult:** when dry, paint clay with
   clear gloss enamel or lacquer.

Rocks can also be painted
and lacquered, and used
as paperweights.

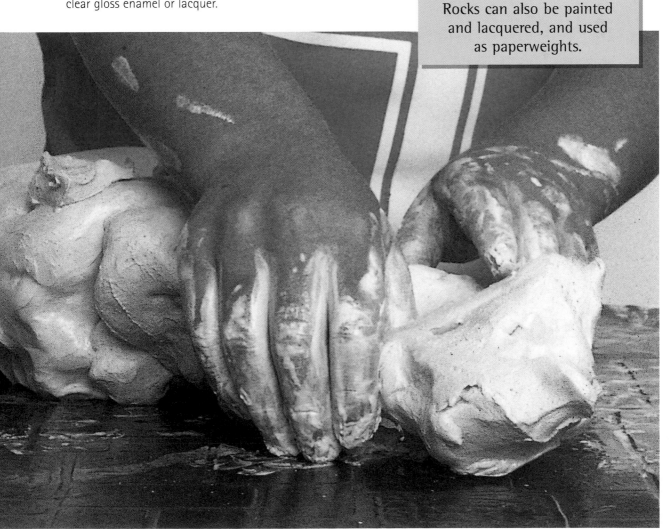

puppets

Few crafts come to life as delightfully as handcrafted puppets. They encourage self-expression, promote interaction with play partners and help to develop social and communication skills. Some children can communicate more easily through their puppet character in a pretend world. The puppets in these projects are made by techniques ranging from papier-mâché to simple sewing. Larger puppets are best tackled by a group of children. A good follow-up activity is to devise and perform a puppet play.

OVER 8 YEARS

glove puppet

you will need
fabric, felt and fur scraps,
    wool, buttons, beads or
    feathers, as desired
PVA glue or needle and thread
plain, long or short glove
fabric crayon
scissors

1 Ask children about the type of
   glove puppet they would like
   to make. Animal pictures may
   provide inspiration and ideas;
   our puppet was created from a
   picture of a panda. Imaginary
   creatures can also be created.
2 Glue or stitch felt, wool, fur or
   buttons onto the glove to create
   the puppet you desire.

   Children might like to create a
   group of animals and have a
   different creature on each finger.

All you need is an old glove, fabric scraps, a
needle and thread, and a little imagination.

sock puppet

OVER 8 YEARS

you will need
sock
thin black cardboard
PVA glue
felt
buttons
needle and thread
scissors

1 Cut a slit in the sock, from the small toe area to the large toe area.
2 Cut a cardboard rectangle about 7cm (2¾in) x 20cm (8in) and curve the corners. (The rectangle should be able to fit into the sock.)
3 Fold the cardboard rectangle in half to form the inside of the mouth. Place the cardboard inside the slit of the sock, aligning the rounded edge with sock edge. Glue in place.
4 Decorate your puppet to create an animal or fantasy creature by stitching on felt shapes for body features such as tongue, ears or nose, and sew on buttons for eyes.

Place the folded cardboard rectangle in the slit of the sock, aligning the rounded edge with the sock edge. Glue the cardboard in place.

easy sock puppet

OVER 3 YEARS

you will need
sock
PVA glue or fabric glue or darning needles threaded with wool (children over five years may be able to use large sewing needles)
felt, ribbon, wool and fabric scraps
buttons
feathers, sequins

1 Put hand inside sock to prevent sewing or gluing both sides of the sock together.
2 Glue or sew on any of the materials to create an animal or person out of the sock. Plastic eyes or buttons are excellent for eyes.

`walking´ puppets

you will need
children's drawings
cardboard
PVA glue
scissors

Glue the drawing onto a piece of cardboard.

2 **Adult:** cut out the drawing, leaving a base of at least 8cm (3¼in) deep. Cut two holes about 1cm (³⁄₈in) apart in the bottom of drawing large enough to slip two fingers through.

3 Put two fingers in the holes for the puppet's legs.

hand puppets

you will need
fabric
felt-tipped pens or fabric pens
  (read directions enclosed)
sewing machine or large needle
  and heavy thread
wool, felt, fabric strips, as desired
scissors

1 Place hand on fabric, spread fingers out and draw around hand with pen. Draw any shape, as long as child's hand fits comfortably into puppet.

2 **Adult:** cut two pieces of fabric about 2cm (³⁄₄in) outside the outline, leaving a wide wrist for the hand to slip into the puppet. Stitch around the outside of the puppet with sewing machine, leaving the wrist open. Alternatively, the child may be able to stitch around the outside of the puppet shape, with a large needle, in running stitch.

3 Sew on coloured wool, felt or fabric strips for animal features. The animal features could be also glued onto the puppet with PVA or fabric glue.

finger puppets

you will need
felt, about 9cm (3½in) x 8cm (3¼in)
sewing machine
fabric scraps, buttons,
     sequins, feathers
PVA or fabric glue
scissors

1 **Adult:** cut two pieces of felt, about
    6cm (2½in) long and 4cm (1½in) wide.
2 **Adult:** place one piece of felt on top of
    the other. Sew a zigzag stitch around the
    felt, making the top rounded and leaving
    the bottom open for finger access.
3 Glue or sew on any fabric scraps, buttons,
    or sequins to create an animal or person.

paper finger puppets

you will need
felt-tipped pens
coloured cardboard
collage materials
PVA glue
adhesive tape
scissors

1 Draw a face or animal shape onto the cardboard, about
    8cm (3¼in) long and 5cm (2in) wide. **Adult:** cut out shape.
2 **Adult:** cut a rectangular strip of cardboard long enough to
    wind around the child's finger, leaving space for glue or tape.
3 Glue or tape ends of strip together to make a circle.
4 Glue back of cut-out drawing onto cardboard circle.
5 Decorate puppet with paper, feathers or other collage materials.

stick puppets

you will need
paint in small bowl
paintbrushes
iceblock sticks
felt-tipped pens

1 Paint a number of iceblock sticks white or any pale colour. (It is harder to paint features on dark coloured sticks.)
2 Draw faces onto sticks. Make a whole family of colourful stick figure puppets.

nature puppets

you will need
stick or branch
pine cone or large seed pod
coconut fibre, small seed pods, moss,
    leaves, seeds
PVA glue

1 Glue or tie stick or branch to appropriate cone or seed pod for head or face of puppet.
2 Glue moss, coconut fibre, leaves or similar materials for hair. Glue seeds for eyes.

stick figure puppets

you will need
children's drawings
cardboard
iceblock sticks
PVA glue
adhesive tape
scissors

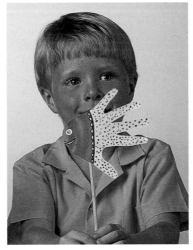

1 Glue drawings onto cardboard. Drawing around a hand makes an interesting shape for a child to make into a creature.
2 **Adult:** cut out drawing. Tape iceblock stick to the back of the cardboard. This becomes the handle with which to hold and play-act with the puppet.

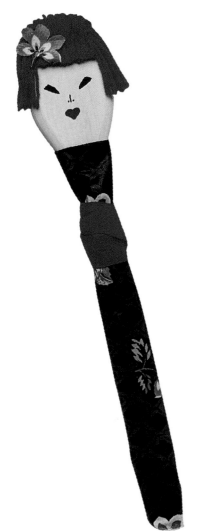

wooden spoons

you will need
wooden spoons
powder paint mixed in small bowl
paintbrushes
wool or cotton wool
felt-tipped pens
fabric scraps
PVA glue

1 Paint wooden spoon white or light colour.
2 Glue wool strands or cotton wool onto spoon for hair. If using wool strands it is easier to glue wool around the edge of spoon across the top and then add another layer running from front to back.
3 Paint or draw face onto spoon. Inside and outside surfaces are both suitable.
4 Wrap fabric around handle. Secure with glue.

Crepe paper, tissue paper or foil can also be used to cover the handle.

white poodle

you will need

15 or more thin white plastic
   shopping bags
rectangular polystyrene piece
old ballpoint pen
thick white sock
4 rubber bands
black or pink felt-tipped pen
newspaper
2 plastic teaspoons
pink fabric scrap (for tongue)
stiff black plastic, such as a soft
   drink bottle base
star stickers
2 pairs of white pantihose
   or stockings
4 plastic lids, such as those from
   margarine containers
fishing Line
PVA glue
adhesive tape
scissors

The white poodle can be made out of lots of different materials recycled from home.

1 Cut the bottom seam and handles off each shopping bag. Cut the sides of the bag so that you have two pieces. To make the poodle's body, place the polystyrene piece on a flat surface and push the plastic bags into the polystyrene using the flat end of a ballpoint pen. Continue until one side of the polystyrene is well covered. This will be the top side of the poodle.

2 Trim the plastic bag ends so that the coat is approximately the same length all over, but long enough to cover the edges of the polystyrene.

3 Make a nose at the toe of the sock by holding a couple of tucks with a rubber band. Colour the nose black or pink with a felt-tipped pen.

4 Stuff the foot of the sock firmly with balls of newspaper. Make the poodle's topknot by putting a rubber band around the heel of the sock. Stuff more newspaper into the leg of the sock.

5 Draw eyes on plastic teaspoons with a felt-tipped pen. Slip the spoon handles under the rubber band that holds the topknot. Cut a long strip of a plastic bag to make ears. Slip the centre of the plastic strip over the topknot and under the rubber band around the topknot.

6 Cut a strip of pink fabric and slip it under the rubber band at the nose. Trim the tongue to the right length and shape then secure with glue.

7 Place a rubber band over each end of the polystyrene body piece. Loop the neck end of the sock onto the band at one end of the body. Tie a fringed plastic bag around base of neck to hide where it joins the body.

8 Cut a thick strip of black plastic for the collar. Decorate with star stickers and put around the poodle's neck. Secure with tape if necessary.

9 Cut the legs off the pantihose. Tie the pantihose legs through the rubber bands at both ends of the poodle's body so that a leg hangs down on each corner of the body. Cut feet off pantihose.

10 Push a plastic lid inside each leg and knot the pantihose leg under each lid. To hold the lid in place, gather the pantihose above the lid and wrap tape around pantihose.

11 Tie a length of fishing line to the top of head and to rubber band at tail end of body. Hold fishing line to make the poodle walk, sit or stand.

Lay the polystyrene on a flat surface and push plastic pieces into polystyrene using a pen.

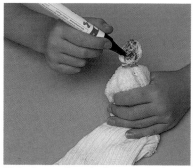

Make the nose by gathering a couple of tucks with a rubber band and colour it black or pink.

The plastic piece for the ears and the spoon eyes slip under the band around the topknot.

Use different
coloured bags
to make a more
colourful poodle.

hamburger puppet

you will need

takeaway hamburger pack

4 strong large rubber bands

pair of coloured tights

2 plastic teaspoons

foil packet

2 paper ring reinforcements
   (coloured with a felt-tipped
   pen) or stickers

plastic bread-wrapper tie

felt-tipped pen

cardboard milk carton

adhesive tape

scissors

Safety first

Keep plastic bread-wrapper
ties out of the reach of small
children as these ties are
extemely dangerous if swallowed.

1 Open the hamburger pack and place two strong rubber bands over each side of the hamburger pack, near the hinge. The puppet's mouth will open and close when fingers and thumb are placed through each band from behind the hinge of the pack.

2 Pull tights over the hamburger pack, from behind the hinge, placing waist inside the pack. Pull a strong rubber band over the tights and across the hinge of the hamburger pack. Legs should hang at each side of the hinge. Cut the tights behind the hinge to make an opening for your hand.

3 **Adult:** make slits at top and front edge of hamburger pack and push teaspoon handles through from top to front edge to make eyes and tusks.

4 Cut the foil packet in a fringe leaving strip attached at one end.

5 Roll up the foil packet and tape in a roll at the intact end.
   Adult: make a small slit in the back of the hamburger pack and push the taped end of the packet through the slit to make the puppet's hair.

6 Place stickers on spoons for eyes or draw with a felt-tipped pen. A bread tie hooked around tights at the front edge, between the puppet's tusks, makes the nose. Draw nostrils on the bread tie with a felt-tipped pen.

7 The legs of the tights make the puppet's legs. Tie knots halfway down the legs to make knees. Cut out some feet from the milk carton. Draw claws on feet with a felt-tipped pen. **Adult:** make a small slit in each foot and push the tights through. Knot the tights under each foot to secure them.

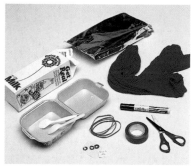

The hamburger puppet can be made from lots of recycled materials found around the house.

Pull two strong rubber bands over the whole of the hamburger pack, near the hinge.

Pull tights over the hamburger pack, from behind the hinge, placing waist inside pack.

Make slits at top and front edge of the pack and push teaspoon handles from top to front.

Roll up foil fringe and tape intact end, then slip it into slit at back of hamburger pack.

Make slits in the milk-carton feet and push legs through slit, then tie a knot under feet.

136   the best of children's art & crafts

cup clown

you will need

large paper cup

paper serviette or tissue paper

star stickers

coloured stickers (for eyes and mouth)

stapler

scissors

1 Cut cup from rim to base in five strips. Cut a piece off the rim end of one strip. The short strip remaining attached to the cup will be the clown's head. Trim the strips on each side of the head to make arms.

2 Trim the piece cut off the head into a triangular shape to make a hat.

3 Cut a piece off the serviette or tissue paper, and cut into thin strips.

4 Staple the thin paper strips to the top of the head to make the clown's hair. Staple the triangular hat over the hair.

5 Cut wide strips of serviette or tissue paper for the frills around the cuffs and neck. Gather strips of paper and staple them onto the clown at the neck, wrists and ankles to make frills. Place a row of stickers down the front of the clown's body and hat. Add other stickers for eyes and mouth.

Cup clown is made from recycled materials.

Cut the serviette into thin strips for the hair.

Thick strips of serviette are for the frills.

Hang the clown from a string or bend his knees to make him sit.

138

net clown

you will need

string
2 small net onion bags
2 patty pan papers
lid from detergent bottle
paper serviette or tissue paper
coloured plastic plate
felt-tipped pen
star stickers
adhesive tape
stapler
scissors

1　Tie one net bag in the middle with string for the legs, allowing a long piece of string to form the hanger.

2　Cut the other bag in half to make arms and tunic. Fold each piece in half and place one on each side of the legs. The cut edge will be the tunic frill.

3　Ask an adult or friend to help tape around the fold (top of the legs) to make the clown's neck, leaving the long string end free at the neck.

4　**Adult:** make a small hole in the centre of two patty pan papers (for the clown's collar), turn them upside down and thread the string through the hole in the papers then through the detergent bottle lid.

5　Cut the cap off the lid. Cut thin strips of serviette or tissue paper and tie the strips tightly in a bundle with the string, making a mop of hair.

6　Cut two feet from the plastic plate and staple to the bottom of each leg.

7　Draw on clown's face with felt-tipped pen. Decorate tunic frill with stars.

Tie a net bag in the middle and cut the other bag in half to make the arms and tunic.

Thread two patty pan papers and bottle lid through the string left free at the neck.

Cut thin strips of serviette and tie strips tightly in a bundle with the string, to form mop of hair.

spider

you will need

soft drink bottle base
red fabric scrap
thread
ballpoint pen
stickers for eyes
felt-tipped pen
stapler
scissors

1 Cut off a strip from around the rim of the bottle base.
2 Cut the strip into eight thin legs.
3 **Adult:** soften the remaining base piece in hot water. Push out the bottom of the base to make it rounded.
4 **Adult:** staple the legs around the edge of the base, positioning them so that they curve out from the body.
5 Cut the fabric scrap into strips and tie in a bundle with thread. Punch two holes in the base with a ballpoint pen. Insert a length of thread through the holes. Tie the bundle of fabric strips over the holes to make hair.
6 Add stickers for eyes. Draw details with felt-tipped pen.

Cut a strip from around the rim of bottle base.

Cut the bottle base strip into eight thin legs.

Push softened base out so that it's rounded.

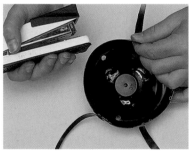

Staple the legs around base so they curve out.

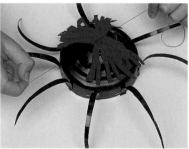

Tie bundle of strips over the holes to make hair.

cuppa snake

you will need

ballpoint pen
30 coloured plastic cups
pantihose leg or a stocking
newspaper
2 coloured plastic plates
felt-tipped pen
paper fasteners or stapler
fishing line, if desired
stick, if desired
scissors

1 Using a ballpoint pen, punch a hole in the base of each cup. Thread cups onto the pantihose leg through the hole in the cup base. To space cups apart, place a ball of newspaper into each cup after it is threaded.

2 For the head, cut the rim off a plastic plate and punch two holes in eye positions with a ballpoint pen. Punch a large third hole at the edge of the plate, above and between the eyes and thread the end of the pantihose through this hole. Thread the pantihose end through the base of another cup which will be a hat. Secure head and hat by tying a knot in pantihose.

3 Cut the base off two plastic cups to make eyes. Draw on the eyes with a felt-tipped pen. Attach each base to plate with paper fasteners or stapler. Cut a strip from second plastic plate shaped like a tongue. Punch a hole and attach tongue underneath head using a paper fastener.

4 Cut a triangular plastic piece from the plate for the tail tip. Punch a hole through the wide end of the plastic piece and thread it onto the end of the snake's tail. Knot the pantihose at the tail end to secure the tail.

To make a moving snake, punch holes at three points along the snake. Attach a piece of fishing line at each point, and tie the other end of each piece to the stick. Shake the stick and the snake will wriggle.

Cuppa snake is made from recycled materials.

Space cups apart with balls of newspaper.

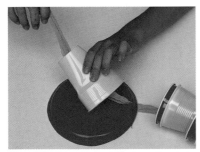

Thread pantihose through final cup for a hat.

OVER 5 YEARS

wriggling snake

you will need
plastic plate
stickers
felt-tipped pen
plastic cup
stapler
thread
scissors

1 Cut a spiralling strip from around the rim of the plastic plate until the plate is about half the original size. Keeping the strip attached, cut a head shape from the centre of the plate.

2 Trim the snake's neck and head until you are happy with the shape. Add stickers for eyes and draw a mouth with a felt-tipped pen. Cut a tongue from the plastic cup. Staple the tongue onto the head. Tie a thread around the neck of the snake. Use it to hang the snake or to make the snake wriggle. If the snake's head won't sit flat it can be cut off and stapled on.

Cut a spiralling strip from rim of plastic plate.

Using a felt-tipped pen, decorate the snake's body with diamonds or stripes

box head puppet

you will need

scrap cardboard, cylinders, cones

empty film canisters, if desired

large cardboard box (head)

paint in small bowls

paintbrushes

paper streamers

thin dowel rod about
    50cm (20in) (shoulders)

70cm (2½ft) cotton tape

thumb tacks

thick dowel rod about 1.8m (6ft)
    (centre rod)

old long-sleeve men's shirt

pair of gloves

fibre filling or crumpled paper

2 dowel rods about 90cm (3ft)
    (arm controls)

PVA glue

masking tape

stapler

scissors

1 Using scrap cardboard, cylinders or cones, make the puppet's nose, mouth, ears and eyes. We used empty film canisters for eyeballs and fringes of cardboard for eyelashes. Glue or tape these facial features onto the box-head, leaving the bottom of the box open.

2 Paint the head with bright paint. Glue on the paper streamers for hair.

3 Tape the shoulder dowel across and at right angles to the centre rod, about 40cm (16in) from the top end of the rod.

4 Cut cotton tape in half. Using a thumb tack, attach the lengths of tape to each end of the shoulder rod. Tape the centre rod securely inside the box at the front side of the head, positioning base of head near shoulder rod.

5 Dress puppet in shirt, threading shoulder rods and arm tapes through the sleeves. Trim both arm tapes until they are the same length as the sleeves.

6 To make hands, stuff each glove with fibre filling or crumpled paper and staple these to the end of the arm tapes. Glue sleeves to the top of the hands. Tie arm control rods to the free ends of each tape.

Two or three people can operate this puppet. One person controls the centre rod with that person's legs becoming the legs of the puppet. One or two people control the arm rods.

Cardboard scraps and cardboard cylinders make the puppet's facial features.

Tape the thin shoulder dowel across and at right angles to the thick centre rod.

cylinder puppet

you will need
fabric pencil or pen
felt, pink and contrasting colours
long cardboard cylinder
cardboard scraps
fabric scraps
wool or raffia
buttons
PVA glue
scissors

1 Using a child's hand as a guide, draw a three-fingered hand shape onto the felt. Cut out the felt making the piece at least 3cm (1¼in) larger than the child's hand.

2 Cut the cardboard cylinder into three pieces; one 7cm (2¾in) long and two 5cm (2in) long. Glue the two short pieces to the outer finger and thumb sections of the felt hand; these will make the puppet's hands. Glue the centre finger section inside the 7cm-long cylinder to make the puppet's head.

3 Cover the head cylinder with pink felt. Glue on a rolled felt strip for the puppet's nose. Cut out two hand shapes from pink felt and glue them inside the hand cylinder.

4 Cut legs and shoes from cardboard and cover in fabric or felt. Glue onto main felt piece.

5 Cut clothes from fabric scraps and wool. Use felt scraps and buttons for facial features. Make hair from wool or raffia and glue onto the head cylinder. The girl puppet's hair was made by taking a bundle of yarns and plaiting at each end, leaving an unplaited section in the centre. The boy's hair is raffia.

> Make cylinder puppets based on characters from a favourite storybook and use the puppets to tell the story.

Use contrasing colours for felt and brightly coloured fabric scraps to dress up the puppets.

Glue the two short cyclinders onto back of arms and the long cylinder into the head.

Cover head cylinder with pink felt and cut out pink hands and glue into short cylinders.

OVER 8 YEARS

broom puppet

you will need

broom or mop

dowel rod about 60cm (24in)

felt-tipped pens

cardboard

buttons, fringe, chenille sticks
(for facial features)

old long-sleeve men's shirt

2 pieces of cord or string, about
50cm (20in) long

2 dowel rods about 90cm (36in)

masking tape

PVA glue

stapler

scissors

1 Stand the broom or mop bristle-end up. Tape the small dowel across the broom handle below the bristle end to make a t-shape. This will form the shoulders of the puppet.

2 Draw a large face shape on cardboard. Cut out the face shape. Tape the face shape to the broom handle so that the bristles or mop top stick out above the face like hair.

3 Glue on a cardboard shape for nose. Add button eyes, fringing for eyebrows, chenille sticks for ears and draw facial features as desired.

4 Dress puppet in the shirt. Cut two hands from cardboard. Staple a hand and a piece of cord (at about halfway down the cord) to each sleeve cuff.

5 Tie the cord to one of the remaining dowel rods. Repeat for other hand. Two children can move the puppet, one operating the arm-control rods; however it's easier with three children, one on each rod.

Tape the small dowel across the broom handle
below the bristle end to make a t-shape.

Tape the face shape to the broom handle so
that the bristles or mop top stick out like hair.

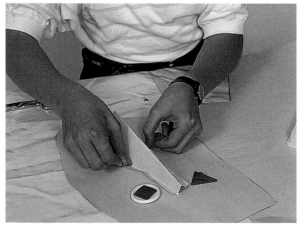

Glue a cardboard nose shape onto the face
and add puppet facial features as desired.

Staple a cardboard hand shape to sleeve cuff
then staple the cord to the sleeve cuff.

Try making other faces to attach to the broom; have a different set of clothing for each character.

OVER 5 YEARS

shadow puppet play

you will need
wire coat-hangers
crayon or pencil
cardboard
plain light-coloured bed sheet
light source (desk lamp, porta flood, etc)
masking tape
scissors

1 **Adult:** straighten out a wire coat-hanger (you shouldn't need to untwist the hanger end) to make a long handle. Wrap tape around the sharp end to prevent injury.

2 Using a crayon or pencil, draw an outline of an animal, person or creature on cardboard. Facial and body details are not needed, although an eye hole is a good detail to include. Inspiration for children's drawings can be provided by animal photographs or pictures.

3 Cut around the character and cut out eyes. Tape the character onto the coat-hanger at the taped end.

4 Make a screen by hanging the bed sheet over a rope or rods, or by fixing it at each corner.

5 Use the puppet between a light source and the fabric screen, while the audience looks on from the other side of the screen.

Draw an outline of the puppet on the cardboard and also draw an eye shape.

Cut around the character and cut out the eye, then tape the character to a coat-hanger.

monster puppet

you will need

large foam block or small pieces
   glued together (for head)

thin foam piece (for teeth)

iceblock sticks

paint in small bowls

paintbrushes

50cm (20in) red felt or fabric
   piece (for tongue)

3 metres (3 yards) of 115cm-wide
   (45in) calico (for body)

fabric strips, yarn, fringing

3 hoops (cane or plastic) or
   6 metres (20ft) garden hose

1.5 metres (1½ yards) cotton tape

thick wool and darning needle,
   if desired

PVA glue

Stanley knife or electric knife

scissors

1 **Adult:** using scissors, Stanley knife or electric knife, carve a head shape from the foam block. Cut chunks from the block to give it a lumpy texture.

2 **Adult:** carve a hollow to fit the child's head in the under section of the monster head. Glue or tie another piece of foam to form the mouth or cut an opening in the large block. (We tied cotton tape around the head and folded a thin rectangular piece of foam over the tape.)

3 Cut a zigzag pattern from a thin foam piece to make teeth. Glue this piece to the inside of the mouth. Glue on foam pieces for eyes. Add iceblock sticks for eyelashes. (Ping pong balls could be used for eyeballs, if desired.)

4 Paint the monster's head in suitable colours. Tie or glue the felt or fabric piece inside the mouth. Cut into shape for tongue.

5 Decorate the body by making small cuts in the calico and tying fabric strips or fringing through the cuts. Fabric strips can be plaited, have buttons tied on, or just left hanging. The body could also be painted.

6 **Adult:** cut hoops in half; or if using garden hose, cut six 1 metre (39in) lengths and bend into a semi-circle.

7 Cut the cotton tape into six equal lengths. Position hoop or hose pieces at regular intervals under the body fabric. Make slits in the fabric and thread the cotton tape through the slits to secure the hoop pieces to the fabric. The hoops shape the body and provide handholds for operators.

8 Tie, glue or stitch body fabric to the back of the head. Tie or stitch fringing at the back of the head for the mane or attach extra fabric strips or yarn. To operate the monster puppet, each child holds a hoop and one child stands underneath the head.

To make a dragon, add a strip of zigzag spine down the puppet's back and decorate the body fabric with fabric cut into the shape of scales.

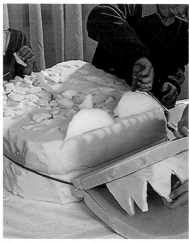

We attached the mouth by tying cotton tape around the head and folding a thin rectangular piece of foam over the tape.

Tie or glue the felt or fabric piece inside the mouth, then cut a shape in the tongue. We cut ours into a three-pronged tongue.

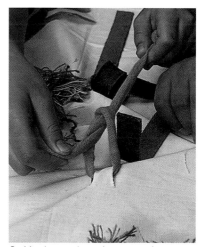

Position hoop or hose pieces at regular intervals under fabric, then thread cotton tape through slits and tie around hoop to secure.

The monster can be used at parades, festivals, school fetes and plays.

OVER 5 YEARS

starfish

you will need

round clear plastic container,
   such as a take-away
   food container
tissue paper
thread
stickers
felt-tipped pen
stapler
PVA glue
scissors

1 Cut the side of the plastic container from the base. Cut five triangles from the side piece of the container.
2 Staple triangles around base of container to make the starfish.
3 Cover the starfish in glue. Lay the starfish onto tissue paper and bunch up the paper to give a bumpy texture. Fold and glue the overhanging paper onto the starfish body so the outline shows clearly. Add more paper if you want a thicker starfish.
4 When the glue is dry, staple a hanging thread to the starfish. Add stickers for eyes and draw details with a felt-tipped pen.

Staple the five triangles onto the starfish.

Hang the starfish or jellyfish near a window so the light shines through it.

jellyfish

you will need

round clear plastic lid, such as
   from a take-away
   food container
tissue paper
thread
stickers
felt-tipped pen
stapler
PVA glue
scissors

1 Cut the plastic lid in half.
2 Glue the lid halves together with the top sides facing out.
3 Cover the lid with glue on both sides. Cut a large rectangular piece of tissue paper. Fold tissue paper in half, then open. Lay the lid in the centre of the paper next to the paper fold. Fold tissue paper over the lid.
4 Glue and fold the paper around the curved edge of the lid. Bunch and gather the paper to give a bumpy texture. Leave about 10cm (4in) of paper hanging free from the straight edge of the lid. Cut the paper at the straight edge of the lid into strips to make tendrils. When the glue is dry, staple a hanging thread to the jellyfish. Add stickers for eyes and draw details with a felt-tipped pen.

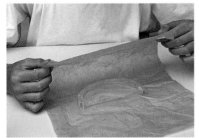

Place the lid halves with the rounded edge close to the centre fold in the tissue paper.

Bunch paper to give a bumpy texture, leaving paper hanging free at straight edge of lid.

Cut the tissue paper at the straight edge of the lid into strips to make the tendrils.

celebrations

Celebrations are exciting and joyous times for children and they'll adore being involved in the preparations. Piñatas, party masks, musical instruments and sweet treats are sure to make that birthday party extra special. Bunnies, bonnets and decorated eggs make great projects for Easter, while Christmas trimmings and decorations encourage children to explore creativity in Christmas themes.

155

musical instruments

rhythm sticks

you will need
paint in small bowls
paintbrushes
2 dowel rods about 30cm (12in) long and
    1cm (⅜in) to 2cm (¾in) thick
clear gloss enamel

1 Paint dowel rods. Leave to dry.
2 **Adult:** coat sticks with clear gloss
    enamel. Hit sticks in time to music.

*The photograph below shows children with, from back, rhythm sticks,
balloon shaker, tambourine, string instrument , bell and paper shakers.*

balloon shaker

you will need
papier-mâché balloon (see page 161)
½ cup of dried beans, corn, rice or sand
powder paint mixed in small bowls (powder
    paint covers newsprint well)
paintbrushes
clear gloss enamel
masking tape
scissors

1 **Adult:** cut a small hole in the papier mâché
    balloon and puncture the balloon.
2 Put in beans, corn, rice or sand. Put at least
    four layers of masking tape over the hole.
3 Paint shaker with white paint (to prevent
    newsprint showing through) and allow to dry.
    Paint with bright colours and allow to dry.
4 **Adult:** coat balloon shaker with clear gloss
    enamel to stop the paint rubbing off.

string instrument

you will need
heavy small box without lid
  (shoe box is a good size)
paint in small bowls
paintbrushes
collage materials
rubber bands of different
  thicknesses and widths

1 Decorate box with paint and
  collage materials. Allow to dry.
2 Put rubber bands around box.
  To play, strum the rubber bands.

tambourine

you will need
2 plastic plates or 3 uncoated
  paper plates
paint in small bowls
paintbrushes
wool
metal bottle caps with a hole
  punched in them (or seashells
  or similar noisy items)
crepe paper or coloured tissue
  paper streamers
PVA glue
hole puncher
tape or stapler

1 Glue plates together for added
  strength. Paint paper plates.
2 **Adult:** punch holes around rim
  of plate, about 5cm (2in) apart.
3 Thread wool through holes
  around plate, adding two
  bottle caps at a time in
  five or six places.
4 **Adult:** tie the ends of the
  wool together in a knot.
5 Tape or staple crepe paper or
  tissue streamers around wool.

silver guitar

This is a more sophisticated version
of the string instrument and is
suited to children over 5 years.

you will need
strong cardboard box, similar size
  to a shoe box (for body)
cardboard cylinder, about 35cm
  (14in) in length (for neck)
foil
cardboard (for head of guitar)
long rubber bands (to fit length
  of cardboard box)
2 old pencils
gift-wrapping ribbon
adhesive tape
scissors

1 **Adult:** cut a hole in lid of box
  leaving about a 5cm (2in) strip
  at sides and 3cm (1¼in) strip
  at top and bottom. Or cut three
  rectangular shapes, as pictured.
2 **Adult:** cut a hole in one end of
  box large enough to fit cardboard
  cylinder through (for the neck).
3 **Adult:** Cover neck with foil.
  Place neck through hole in box
  and tape it in place. For tuning
  screws, make six small balls of
  foil, and attach three each side

to the top of the neck with
looped pieces of tape. Cut a
triangle out of the cardboard and
cover with foil. Make two slits in
top of neck, above tuning screws,
and slide triangular piece in to
make the head of the guitar.
4 Tape lid to box. Cover box with
  foil. Cut foil from hole in lid,
  leaving some foil to tuck in hole.
5 Stretch the rubber bands,
  lengthways, over the box.
6 Place pencils covered in
  foil under the bands at each
  end to give a better sound.
7 Tie curling ribbon (strap) around
  neck of guitar and secure at
  bottom of box with tape.

bell shaker

you will need
cardboard cylinder, about
  15cm (6in) long
tissue paper
liquid starch
wool
metal jingle bells
hole puncher

1 **Adult:** punch holes 1cm (⅜in)
  apart around one end of cylinder.

2 Decorate cylinder with tissue
  paper applied with liquid
  starch. Allow to dry.
3 Thread the wool through
  holes in the cylinder and
  adding a bell between each
  wool loop.
4 **Adult:** tie ends of wool in a knot.

For variation, glue or staple foil
or paper streamers to one end of
cylinder to make a paper shaker.

coconut clappers

you will need

coconut
paint in small bowls
paintbrushes
clear gloss enamel

1 **Adult:** cut a coconut shell in half and remove flesh.
2 Paint the coconut shell halves with bright colours.
3 **Adult:** paint coconut halves with clear gloss enamel. To play, the child holds a coconut half in each hand and claps them together.

bottle shakers

you will need

½ cup dried beans, corn or rice
plastic drink bottle with lid
collage materials, or tissue paper
   and liquid starch
PVA glue

1 Put dried beans, corn or other similar items into empty plastic bottles. Replace lid.
2 Decorate with collage materials and PVA glue or tissue paper applied with liquid starch.

pie plate shakers

Younger children may need help with sewing.

you will need

foil pie plates (put one plate inside
   another for strength if they are thin)
coloured wool on darning needle with
   knot tied in end
funnel
dried beans or other dried food
cut paper shapes (see pages 183 and 184) or
   any collage materials
PVA glue

1 Place a plate right-side up and place second plate on top, right-side down. Stitch around outside with wool about 1cm (³/₈in) apart, leaving opening. Use funnel to pour beans inside. Sew up opening.
2 Glue on paper shapes or collage materials.

Stitching a pie plate shaker.

coconut clappers

bottle shakers

drum

you will need

brown wrapping paper
empty tin can with lid cut off
paper paste
white paper
collage materials, foil, tissue paper or
    children's old drawings
paint in small bowls, if desired
paintbrushes
saucepan lid, larger than tin
masking tape
scissors

1 Place saucepan lid on wrapping paper
   and trace around it. Trace about eight
   more circles and cut them out.
2 Place a circle of paper over open end
   of can. Fold paper around sides of
   can and tape into place.
3 Brush paper paste onto paper and place
   another circle of paper on top and tape
   into place around sides of can. Repeat
   until top is strong (usually eight or nine
   layers). Allow to dry.
4 Cover can with white paper and secure
   with tape. Decorate with collage materials,
   foil, children's drawings or paint.

To make a drumstick: Cover top of
tablespoon with cotton wool. Cover cotton
wool with piece of fabric, about 10cm (4in)
square, and secure with rubber bands.

drums & drumstick

xylophone

you will need

6 glass fruit juice or milk bottles
6 food colours
pencil or spoon

1 Fill bottles with water to varying levels.
2 Add a different food colour to each bottle.
   Gently strike each bottle with a pencil or
   spoon to get different notes.

xylophone

OVER 4 YEARS

paper bag piñata

Real piñatas, made from pottery and originating in Mexico, are centrepieces at celebrations. They are filled with sweets, tiny presents, flowers and other treasures. When hit with a stick, piñatas explode into fragments and shower their contents into the uplifted hands of party guests. For children, piñatas are made to be broken more easily, as on this page, with the simple paper bag example. More sturdy piñatas, using papier-mâché techniques, are on the right.

you will need
newspaper
paper bags
string, about 1 metre (1 yard)
   in length
powder paint mixed in small bowls
   (powder paint covers newsprint)
paintbrushes
tissue paper
paper paste or liquid starch
crepe paper
sweets
blindfold
stick, about 1 metre (39in) in length
   and 3cm (1¼in) thick
scissors

1 Scrunch up the newspaper. Fill paper bag with the newspaper to make the bag firm so it is easier to paint. Tie the end of the paper bag with string.
2 Cover paper bag with paint and/or tissue paper applied with paste or liquid starch. If desired, take crepe paper and fold several times to form a 5cm (2in) strip. On one fold make repeated 3cm (1¼in) cuts close together. Run fingers across loops to separate them a little. With loops pointing up, glue uncut side around bag. Allow to dry.
3 Untie end of bag and remove newspaper. Fill bag with sweets; retie string.
4 **Adult:** tie bag to ceiling with string, keeping bag well down from ceiling so as not to cause any damage with stick. Child wearing a blindfold stands near piñata and swings at it with stick, trying to break it open. After four or five attempts, the blindfold and stick should be given to another child to try and break piñata. When piñata breaks open, sweets will fall out for children to collect. All spectators should stand well clear of the child with the stick! At a party, it is a good idea to have one piñata for every four children so that each child gets a turn at trying to break it.

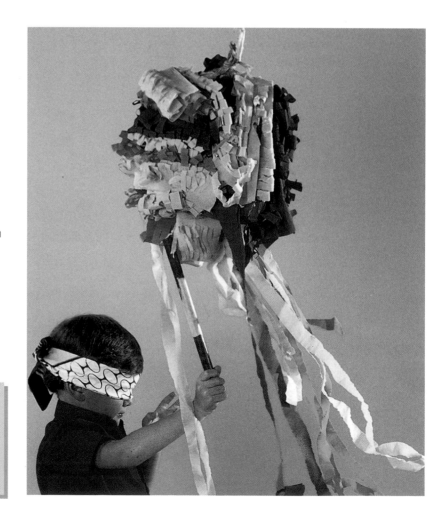

The paper bag piñata is very simple to make. Other good party ideas: face painting, dressing up and treasure hunts.

papier-mâché fish piñata

you will need
balloon
coloured newsprint or newspaper
paper paste (see page 5)
powder paint mixed in
   small bowls
paintbrushes
strips of crepe and
   cellophane paper
collage materials
masking tape
sweets
scissors

1 **See steps 1 and 2 below.**
3 Paint piñata with bright
   colours, to make fish, bird,
   animal or abstract creation.
   Tape on crepe streamers
   and collage materials for
   decoration. Leave piñata to dry.
4 **Adult:** cut a small lid in the top,
   prick balloon and pull it out. Fill
   hollow with sweets. Tape hole up.

papier-mâché balloon

you will need
balloon
newspaper
paper paste (see page 5)
powder paint mixed in small
   bowls (powder paint covers
   newsprint well)
paintbrushes
lacquer or clear gloss enamel

1 Blow up balloon and tie a double knot
   in the end.
2 Tear newspaper into strips. Place a
   strip into paper paste and cover
   completely with paste. Take strip from
   paste and wrap it around balloon.
   Repeat process until balloon has about
   three layers of paper around it. Allow to
   dry thoroughly (it takes one or two days,
   depending on the layers of newspaper).
3 Paint a colourful design on the balloon.
   Allow to dry thoroughly.
4 **Adult:** coat papier-mâché balloon with
   lacquer or clear gloss enamel.

Dip newspaper strip in paste so strip is completely covered, then cover balloon with strip. Repeat until balloon has three layers.

circle masks

you will need
felt-tipped pens
cardboard
large plate or saucepan lid
paint in small bowls
paintbrushes
crepe paper or wool
elastic
PVA glue
scissors

1 Draw a circle on cardboard using a large plate or saucepan lid. **Adult:** cut out circle. Make incision from edge to centre and overlap pieces to form a slight peak in centre of cardboard. Glue overlapping pieces together. Paint cardboard a colour for skin or fur of a human or animal face. Allow to dry.
2 **Adult:** cut strips of crepe paper or wool for hair. Glue to top edges of mask.
3 Paint or draw a face on outside of paper plate.
4 **Adult:** cut holes for eyes and mouth and also at side of mask to thread elastic through. Thread elastic and tie around back of child's head.

Children enjoy dressing up and pretending they are someone else and masks help them to take on a new personality.

piggy mask

you will need
lid of spray can
paper plate
paint in small bowls
paintbrushes
cardboard
felt-tipped pens
elastic
PVA glue
masking tape
scissors

1 Tape lid of spray can to lower half of paper plate.
2 Paint paper plate pink or light colour. Allow to dry.
2 **Adult:** cut out two ear shapes from the cardboard and glue to back of mask.
3 Paint or draw a face on front of mask.
4 **Adult:** cut holes for eyes and mouth and at side of mask to thread elastic through. Thread elastic and tie around back of child's head.

new faces

you will need
face pictures, cut from magazines
light cardboard
iceblock sticks
glue
masking tape
scissors

1 Glue pictures onto cardboard. **Adult:** carefully trim around the picture. Use eyes, nose and mouth to make separate masks or use the whole face. Small lookout holes can be cut out for eyes. Older children can find and cut out their own pictures.
2 Tape a stick onto the back of each mask, at the side or bottom.

celebrations 163

OVER 8 YEARS

papier-mâché mask with clay mould

you will need

block of clay (see page 6)

thin plastic wrap

newspaper or telephone
   book pages

glue mixture (½ PVA glue +
   ½ water)

container for glue mixture

paint in small bowls

paintbrushes

fringed fabric strips (for hair)

cord

1 Working on a plastic- or
newspaper-covered tabletop,
mould the clay to form the face
of a person or animal.

2 Cover the clay mould with plastic
wrap, making sure it clings
closely to the clay.

3 Tear paper into small pieces. Dip
newspaper pieces into the glue
mixture and place on the plastic-
wrapped clay mould. Smooth
paper pieces so that there are
no air bubbles or lumps.
Continue adding glue-dipped
newspaper until you have
built up four or five layers.
Leave to dry overnight.

4 Remove the mask from the clay
mould then paint and decorate as
desired. We glued on fabric strips
for hair. For hanging, punch holes
at each side and attach a cord
across the back of the mask.

On a covered tabletop, work the clay into the face of a person, fantasy creature or animal.

A face with large and distinct features will work well for the papier-mâché mask.

Cover the clay mould with plastic wrap, making sure it clings closely to the clay.

Dip the newspaper strips into the glue mixture and place on the plastic-wrapped clay mould.

Continue adding the glue-dipped newspaper until you have built up four or five layers.

When the mask is dry remove it from the clay mould, then paint and decorate as desired.

Pictures of tribal or carnival masks
will provide lots of inspiration!

OVER 10 YEARS

plaster bandage mask

you will need
plaster bandage
Vaseline
container of water
paint in small bowls
paintbrushes
ribbon or cord
scissors

> Use the mask as a wall decoration when it's not being worn.

1 This activity should be carefully supervised by an adult. Cut the plaster bandage into strips approximately 4cm (1½in) long.

2 **Adult supervision:** tie back the child's hair and generously coat the face with Vaseline so that the mask can be removed easily.

3 Dip a bandage strip in water and place it on child's face. Smooth the bandage strip so that there are no air bubbles or bumps.

4 **Adult supervision:** avoiding the nostrils, mouth and eyes, continue applying the bandage strips, overlapping each bandage strip until the entire face is well covered.

5 Strengthen the mask by adding another layer of plaster bandage. To remove the mask, gently lift the edges to break the suction, then carefully lift the mask from the face. Let the mask dry completely.

6 Trim uneven edges and paint as desired. Make a hole at each side of the face and thread ribbon or cord through to make mask ties.

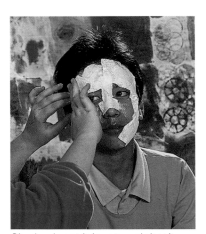

Dip a bandage strip in water and place it on child's face, then smooth out the strip.

Continue the plastering process but be careful to avoid the child's nostrils, mouth and eyes.

The mask should have a couple of layers of bandage strips to give it added strength.

To remove the mask, gently lift the edges of the mask to break the suction.

Let the mask dry completely, then trim the edges and paint and decorate as desired.

chicken wire mask

you will need
wire cutters
chicken wire
newspaper or telephone book
glue mixture (½ PVA glue + ½ water)
PVA glue
powder paint mixed in small bowls
paintbrushes
fringing or curled paper for hair
foam, if desired
masking tape
scissors

1 **Adult:** cut and shape the chicken wire into a large head shape that can easily slip over the child's head and rest on their shoulders. Cover wire ends with tape for safety.

2 Tear newspaper or telephone book pages into large pieces. Dip large pieces of newspaper into the glue mixture and then place these onto the chicken wire until it is completely covered with the paper.

3 Roll and crumple newspaper to form nose, mouth, forehead ridge, eyebrows and eyeballs. Glue features in place. We cut out ear shapes from thin cardboard.

4 Continue applying glue-dipped newspaper over features and face until you have built up about four layers. Allow to dry overnight.

5 Paint over the newsprint with white or pale powder paint. Paint facial features as desired. Glue fringing or curled paper onto head for hair.

6 If necessary, pad the inside of the mask with foam for comfort.

7 **Adult:** cut one or two lookout holes for wearer. These do not have to be in the same position as the puppet's eyes.

Cut and shape a large head that can slip over child's head and sit on the shoulders.

Tear newspaper or telephone book pages into large pieces and dip in glue mixture.

Place large glue-dipped paper pieces on the chicken wire head and smooth out bumps.

Apply glue-dipped paper pieces over features and face until there are four layers.

Let mask dry overnight, then paint over the newsprint with white or pale powder paint.

Paint and decorate the mask as desired and glue on fringing or curled paper for hair.

Create and use masks for a school play or write a play around the characters you make.

treats to eat

rice bubble creatures

you will need
50g butter or margarine
250g marshmallows
2–3 cups of Rice Bubbles
currants, glacé cherries, licorice,
    peppermints, candied
    citrus pieces
chenille sticks
frying pan
spoon
foil

1 **Adult:** melt butter/margarine in frying pan on low heat. Add marshmallows and continue stirring until marshmallows are melted, or microwave together on high for 2 minutes
2 **Adult:** while stirring, add enough Rice Bubbles to make a stiff consistency (approximately 2–3 cups). Remove from heat.
3 Tear off large pieces of foil (about 30cm (12in)) for each child. Lightly grease foil.
4 Put a little butter on inside of hands. While mixture is just warm (not hot), mould into desired shape. Decorate as desired with dried fruit and chenille sticks.

sweet insects
you will need
sweets, such as freckles, licorice all-sorts,
    candy-coated chocolates, candy bananas
clear plastic wrap
coloured chenille sticks

1 Place sweets on strips of plastic wrap and wind the wrap around them to form shapes.
2 Twist chenille sticks at appropriate intervals to form head, bodies and legs. These quaint creatures are great for birthday party table decorations or for hanging with other baubles on the Christmas tree.

dried fruit figures

snake

you will need

chenille stick

12 prunes

glacé cherry

orange peel

1 Thread chenille stick through prunes.
2 Decorate snake's head with glacé cherry for eyes and orange peel for tongue.

spider

you will need

chenille sticks

dried fig

prune

slivered almonds

glacé cherry

scissors

1 **Adult:** cut chenille sticks in half. Insert four sticks into each side of dried fig to make the legs.
2 **Adult:** cut a 2cm (³⁄₈in) long piece of chenille stick to attach the head to the body. Pierce half the chenille stick into the dried fig. Attach the prune to the other end of the chenille stick.
3 Decorate with slivered almonds and glacé cherry.

caterpillar

you will need

needle and thread

7 pieces dried apricots

currants

glacé cherry

chenille stick

1 **Adult:** using the needle and thread, string apricots together.
2 Decorate caterpillar with currants for eyes, glacé cherry for mouth and chenille sticks for antennae.

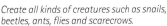

Create all kinds of creatures such as snails, beetles, ants, flies and scarecrows.

bonnets

you will need

children's paintings
collage materials
silk or plastic flowers
crepe paper or coloured wool
PVA glue
stapler
scissors

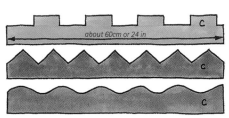

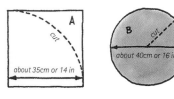

1 Select one of the bonnet patterns shown below left. **Adult:** trace the pattern onto an old painting. Cut bonnet out.
2 Glue collage materials and flowers onto bonnet. Allow to dry.
3 **Adult:** glue or staple crepe paper or wool to each side of bonnet to act as an under-chin tie. For variation, cover bonnet shapes with foil, tissue paper or cellophane before decorating.

Hat A Roll paper into a cone and staple at bottom. Staple a ribbon or crepe paper streamer on each side of bonnet to act as a tie.

Hat B Make a cut from edge of circle to centre. Overlap two pieces by about 8cm (3in) to form a slight peak, similar to a Chinese-style hat. Staple together. Staple ribbons to inside of bonnet.

Hat C Place the cut-out shape around the child's head to get the correct size. Staple the ends of the bonnet together.

note It's easier to decorate bonnets before they are stapled together.

bunnies

you will need
2 polystyrene balls
  (different sizes)
eyes, if desired
felt-tipped pens
chenille sticks
toothpick
cotton wool balls
cardboard
knife
PVA glue
scissors

1 **Adult:** with a knife, cut a slice from bottom of largest ball (body) to make it sit flat. Cut a small slice from top of body and a small slice from bottom of small ball (head). Attach body to head with glue.

2 Glue on eyes and draw mouth onto face. **Adult:** to attach chenille sticks for whiskers, pierce holes in the head with a toothpick, then place chenille sticks into holes. Glue cotton wool balls for legs or draw feet onto cardboard, cut out cardboard and glue to bottom of body. Glue cotton wool balls on for tail and ears.

For variation, draw a bunny onto a piece of cardboard and make a stand for it by taping one end of a rectangular piece of cardboard to the back of the drawing and folding it at a right angle.

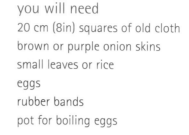

onion skin egg dyeing

you will need
20 cm (8in) squares of old cloth
brown or purple onion skins
small leaves or rice
eggs
rubber bands
pot for boiling eggs

1 Place cloth on table. Place six layers of onion skins on top of cloth. Place leaves or rice on top of onion skins.

2 Place egg on top of skins, leaves and rice and place more onion skins on top. Wrap cloth firmly around egg and onion skins. Wrap a number of rubber bands around the cloth to keep it in place and to press the onion skins firmly against the egg.

3 **Adult:** put the wrapped egg in a pot of boiling water and keep at boiling point for 30 minutes.

4 Remove the egg from the water, leave to cool. Remove cloth and materials. When the egg is dry it can be rubbed with a little cooking oil to give it a shiny appearance.

crayon-resist dyeing

OVER
3
YEARS

you will need

crayons

hard-boiled eggs

vegetable dye or fabric dye or
    crepe paper dye (see page 176)

foil

cup

spoon

1 Draw designs onto eggs with crayons. Heavier crayon lines will
   show up more after dyeing.

2 Following directions on packet, mix up ⅔ of a cup of strong dye in
   a cup or use crepe paper dye as used on batik eggs (see page 176). If
   dye is warm, wait for it to cool (warm dye will melt the crayon wax).

3 Using spoon, put egg into dye. It should be completely covered.
   Carefully lift the egg out to check colour. Leave in dye until desired
   colour is reached (usually a few minutes). Lift egg out with spoon and
   place on a wrinkled piece of foil to dry.

batik eggs

you will need

fresh raw eggs, or whole hard-
   boiled eggs

pin

crepe paper (assorted colours)

hot water

1 tablespoon of white vinegar

candle

matches

spoon

bowl

scissors

We 'blew' raw eggs by making a small hole with a pin in both ends of egg and blowing out the contents (it takes a bit of puff!). This way the yolks and whites can be used in cooking. However, the blown egg is quite fragile and if you prefer, hard-boiled eggs can be used. They should keep indefinitely, as the contents of eggs will dry up without odour, unless the shell cracks.

1 To make the dye, cut strips of crepe paper about 2cm (¾in) wide and place in a bowl. **Adult:** cover with hot water to release the dye.

2 Remove crepe paper from dye with a spoon. Add white vinegar to set dye. Allow dye to cool.

3 **Adult:** the eggs are decorated with several applications of wax and dye. Start with the lightest colour and work to the darkest. If you wish to leave any sections of the eggshell surface its natural colour, drip candle wax onto that area. Dip the egg in the lightest dye (yellow, perhaps). It may take a few minutes to reach the desired colour. Dry with a tissue. **Adult:** drip wax onto the sections you want to keep yellow. Dip egg in the darker dye, until it is the desired colour and dry with a tissue. Repeat the process until you have used all the desired colours.

4 **Adult:** to remove wax, place egg on a tray in a moderate oven. When wax has melted (about two minutes), wipe dry with a tissue.

For variation, make leaf-printed eggs. Take a small piece of fern or ivy and hold it onto the egg. Secure the leaf in place by wrapping a piece of stocking very firmly around the egg. Tie top of stocking with elastic band and dip egg in dye. Remove excess dye with a tissue and, when dry, peel off stocking and leaves to reveal pattern.

Safety first
Adult supervision is necessary as hot water and hot wax are used.

Place strips of crepe paper in a bowl and pour hot water over strips to release the dye.

Leave some of the egg's natural colour by dripping wax on the egg before dipping in dye.

Dip the egg in the yellow dye or if using a shallow dish, spoon the dye over the egg.

Carefully drip the candle wax onto the sections that you want to keep yellow.

With a spoon, dip the egg into the second dye and leave in dye until egg is desired colour.

For the leaf-printed egg, wrap a leaf around the egg and secure leaf with a tight-fitting stocking.

OVER 3 YEARS

Easter baskets

grass Easter basket

Start preparing basket three weeks before the Easter holiday.

you will need
potting soil
plastic container (empty margarine or
    ice-cream container)
lawn seed
paintbrush
liquid starch in a bowl
tissue paper scraps
cord, heavy wool, ribbon or braided
    crepe paper
stapler
scissors, if needed

1 Place a 3cm (1¼in) layer of potting soil in the plastic container. Sprinkle lawn seed thickly on top of soil so that seeds almost touch. Cover seeds with a thin layer of soil.
2 Water seeds lightly as described on seed packet and continue to keep surface moist every day. Place grass basket in a light spot. Leave grass to grow for two weeks.
3 A few days before Easter, paint basket with liquid starch. Cover basket with tissue paper scraps in various shapes. Tissue can be applied in several layers, using the starch as a glue.
4 For handles, staple cord, heavy wool, ribbon or braided crepe paper to each side of basket. Large baskets need two handles for good balance.

foil Easter basket

you will need
foil
plastic container (empty
   margarine or ice-cream
   container)
thick powder paint mixed
   with dishwashing liquid in
   small bowl (see page 6)
paintbrushes
scissors, if needed

1 Place large sheet of foil on table. Put container in middle and bring
   foil up around sides, over top and partially down inside of container.
   Trim excess if necessary. Press foil close to container.
2 Paint designs onto foil. Allow to dry.

note If paint doesn't stick, add more dishwashing liquid. This will
     help it to stick to any slippery surface including plastic or foil.

egg tree

OVER
4
YEARS

you will need
tree branch, about 1 metre (3¼ft)
   in length
bucket of sand
pastel powder paint mixed in bowls
paintbrushes
hard-boiled eggs
felt-tipped pens
pin
chenille sticks
knife
spoon

1 Place branch in bucket of sand. Paint
   branch with pastel paint.
2 **Adult:** cut tops off eggs. With a spoon,
   gently scoop egg out of eggshell.
3 Using paint or felt-tipped pens, colour
   designs on eggshells. Tissue paper may also
   be stuck onto eggshells for decoration.
4 **Adult:** very gently, stick a pin through
   bottom of egg to make a small hole.
   Carefully push a chenille stick through hole.
   Bend end over to keep it inside the egg.
5 Curve end of chenille stick to form a hook.
   Hang the eggs all over the painted branch.

tree decorations

pasta ornaments

you will need
pencil
cardboard
coloured and uncoloured
  pasta shapes (see page 6)
gold or silver spray
  paint, if desired
newspaper, if desired
ribbon
PVA glue
hole puncher
scissors

1 Draw Christmas shapes onto the cardboard.
2 **Adult:** cut out shapes. Glue several identical shapes together for added strength. Punch or make hole in one end of shape.
3 Glue pasta onto one side. If desired, pasta can be glued onto other side. Other appropriate collage materials may be used. Allow glue to dry.
4 **Adult:** if desired, spray ornaments with gold or silver paint. Spread newspaper in well-ventilated area. Lay ornament on newspaper, spray with paint and allow to dry.
5 Thread ribbon through hole and hang ornament on tree.

metal pie plates

you will need
pencil or paintbrush
small foil pie plates
glitter
string or ribbon
PVA glue

1 **Adult:** punch a hole into pie plate with a pencil or the end of a paintbrush.
2 Apply glue to pie plates (either side for different effects). Apply glitter to glued areas. Shake off excess glitter. Allow to dry.
3 Thread ribbon through hole and tie ornament to tree.

For variation, a pattern of holes could be made and threaded with coloured wool or ribbon. Strips of cellophane could also be glued.

egg cup bells

you will need
egg carton
foil
glitter
collage materials
coloured chenille sticks
clear craft glue
scissors

1 **Adult:** cut egg carton into cups.
2 Cut a circle from foil about 15cm (6in) in diameter. Place egg cup in centre of foil circle and wrap foil around it loosely so that irregularities in its shape are not too noticeable. Press gently.
3 Apply glue to foil and sprinkle with glitter. Other collage materials may be glued on but paint cannot be successfully applied to foil that is very wrinkled or lumpy.
4 **Adult:** pierce hole in top of bell with scissors or other sharply pointed instrument.
5 Place a chenille stick through the hole in each bell and bend the end inside so bell will not slip off. A jingle bell can be attached to chenille stick inside. Bend a hook shape into other end and hang the bell on branch of Christmas tree.

hairpin ornaments

you will need
thick paper or cardboard
hairpins
ribbon, about 20cm (8in) long
newspaper
silver or gold spray paint
PVA glue
scissors

1 **Adult:** cut two circles of paper about 3cm (1¼in) in diameter. Put glue in centre of circle and place about eight hairpins onto glue, leaving rounded edges of hairpins touching in centre.
2 Loop ribbon so both ends are touching, then glue ribbon to other paper circle. When glue and hairpins are almost set, place other circle of paper on top of pins, ribbon-side down. Press firmly. Allow ornament to dry.
3 **Adult:** spread newspaper in well-ventilated area. Lay ornament on newspaper and spray with gold or silver paint. Allow to dry. Tie ornament to Christmas tree.

For variation, paint hairpins with glue and roll them in glitter. Make other decorative shapes.

note Children under four years may need help to arrange hairpins.

polystyrene trays

you will need
polystyrene tray
thick powder paint mixed with dishwashing liquid in small bowls (see page 6)
paintbrushes
tissue paper
PVA glue
scissors

1 Cut polystyrene trays into Christmas shapes.
2 Paint trays with powder paint. If the paint will not adhere to part of the tray, add more dishwashing liquid.
3 Glue tissue paper to the shapes. Trim when dry.

Christmas ball

you will need
polystyrene ball
foil
narrow-necked bottle
powder paint mixed with dishwashing liquid in small bowls (see page 6)
paintbrushes

1 Cover polystyrene ball with foil.
2 Set ball on bottle to prevent ball from rolling around. Paint the ball. If paint doesn't adhere add more dishwashing liquid.

glitter ball

you will need
polystyrene ball
glitter
sequins, small beads
pins (with large heads)
ribbon
PVA glue

1 Cover ball with glue. Do not use clear craft glue or spray enamel paint, which dissolve the polystyrene. Roll ball in glitter.
2 **Adult:** put sequin onto pin and insert into ball. Repeat with all sequins and beads.
3 Wrap ribbon around the ball, leaving extra length for hanging. Fasten ribbon with a pin.

'Stained glass' shapes

you will need
tissue paper scraps
sheet of waxed paper
liquid starch
ribbon
hole puncher
scissors

1 Apply tissue paper scraps to waxed paper with liquid starch. Allow papers to dry.
2 Cut Christmas shapes out of the waxed paper. Punch a hole in the top of the shape, insert ribbon through it and hang in front of a light on the Christmas tree.

snowflakes

you will need
colourful squares of thin paper (any size)
scissors

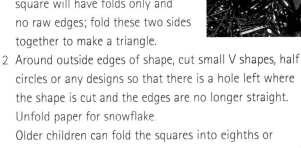

1 Fold a square in half then fold in half again. Two sides of the square will have folds only and no raw edges; fold these two sides together to make a triangle.
2 Around outside edges of shape, cut small V shapes, half circles or any designs so that there is a hole left where the shape is cut and the edges are no longer straight. Unfold paper for snowflake.
Older children can fold the squares into eighths or sixteenths to make a more intricate snowflake. Younger children may need help with cutting folded paper.

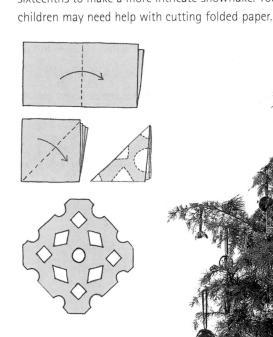

Christmas cards

Old Christmas cards make delightful tree decorations and are easy to do. Simply cut out designs and figures from your favourite old cards, punch a hole through top of cut-out, thread a colourful ribbon through the hole and tie it onto the tree.

pretzel ornaments

you will need
foil, about 15cm (6in) x 20cm (8in)
pretzels
red and green crinkly gift-wrapping ribbon
  or double-sided satin ribbon
PVA glue

1 Place foil on table. Arrange pretzels into a design
   on the foil so that each pretzel touches
   another in at least two places.
2 Place one large drop of glue at each point where
   pretzels touch. When joined, add another drop of glue.
3 Make sure all pretzels are touching in the glued areas.
   Leave on foil. Allow to dry overnight.
4 Remove ornament carefully from foil. Weave ribbon
   through holes. Handle the pretzel gently.

paper stars

you will need
colourful squares of thin paper, about 20cm
  (8in) square
scissors

1 Fold a square in half diagonally to make a
   triangle. Mark the centre point along fold
   (point A). Keeping first fold, fold twice more
   to make a triangle each time.
2 Fold top of triangle (point B) down as shown
   in illustration, taking care to line up folded
   edges evenly along bottom.
3 Cut away shaded area. Open paper out for
   an eight-point star. Cut a jagged line or
   cut curves for flower shapes.

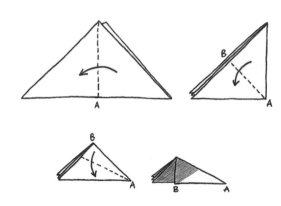

wrapping presents

Paintings and prints make appealing
wrapping paper. Decorate wrapped presents
with snowflakes, which can be glued or
attached with double-sided sticky tape. Wrap
presents in foil and cover with snowflakes
(see page 183) and star shapes (see above).

advent boxes

Advent is the season before Christmas. Advent boxes are small boxes which are filled with sweets and little surprises, wrapped up and numbered from one to 24. As the countdown to Christmas begins on December 1, a present is opened each day until Christmas Eve.

you will need

24 small boxes of varying sizes
sweets, nuts, sultanas or small toys
Christmas paper scraps and children's
    paintings (for wrapping paper)
red and green crinkly
    gift-wrapping ribbon
24 adhesive labels
adhesive tape
pen
scissors

1 Fill each box with sweets, nuts or small toys.
2 Wrap each box individually with wrapping paper and secure box with tape.
3 Tie each box with ribbon and a bow. Curl loose ends of ribbon by holding ribbon firmly between thumb and back of scissors and pulling ribbon through with your free hand.
4 Write a number from one to 24 on each adhesive label. Stick a label on each box.
5 Cut 24cm (9½in) long pieces of ribbon. Tie one end onto each box. Adjust the boxes so they hang at different lengths. Take all the ribbons at the top in one hand and divide them in half. Tie halves together with a double knot and a large bow. Curl all the ends of the loose ribbons. Hang up advent boxes on the Christmas tree.

ALL AGES

candle centrepieces

you will need
uncooked salt play dough (see
recipe, page 9)
foil
wide red candle or several thin
red candles
seed pods with longish
stems, small pine cones,
greenery sprigs
Christmas ribbon
hairpins
silver or gold spray paint
glitter
clear gloss enamel spray
dinner plate

1 Play dough will form the
foundation for the centrepiece.
Put play dough on piece of
foil around a wide red candle
or, for variation, keep play dough
in a wreath shape and stick
thinner red candles into it.
2 Push seed pods and other items
firmly into play dough.
3 If centrepiece is not to be
painted, add ribbons tied in bows
by sticking a hairpin through
back of bow and pushing the
hairpin ends into the dough.
4 **Adult:** if centrepiece is to be
painted, remove candles. In a
well-ventilated area, spray gold
or silver paint onto centrepiece.
Glitter may then be sprinkled on.
Adult: spray glitter with clear
gloss enamel to keep it in place.
5 If desired, fold foil under
dough after it is firm. Move the
centrepiece onto the plate gently.

Be really original and spray seed pods and beetles silver or gold!

ALL
AGES

stained glass window

you will need

black paper

same size sheets waxed
    paper, tracing paper or any
    transparent paper

cellophane or tissue paper torn
    into small pieces about 3cm
    (1¼in) to 8cm (3in)

liquid starch (if using
    tissue paper)

adhesive tape, if needed

PVA glue

scissors

1 **Adult:** fold the black paper into eighths. On a side that has only folds
   (no raw edges), cut out a square as illustrated. When unfolded this
   is the window frame. The frames need not be square shapes.
   Snowflakes (page 183) would be very attractive.

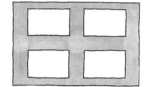

2 Place waxed paper or tracing paper onto table. If it curls, tape corners
   to table. If using tissue paper, apply a little liquid starch to waxed paper
   and place tissue paper on it. If using cellophane, put glue around edges
   and place it on waxed paper. Liquid starch will make cellophane buckle.

3 Glue frame onto the waxed paper or tracing paper. Hang on the window
   for the sun to shine through. Heavy white paper should replace the
   transparent paper if the picture is not to hang on a window.

*If using cellophane, put glue around edges of
piece and place it on the waxed paper.*

*Continue gluing the cellophane pieces until
the wax sheet is completely covered.*

nature wreath

you will need
pencil
large plate and smaller plate
2 sheets heavy cardboard
pine cones, seed pods,
   dried leaves
Christmas ribbon
clear gloss enamel spray
PVA glue
scissors

1 Make a wreath by tracing around large plate on both cardboard sheets. Place smaller plate in centre of drawn circle and trace around it on both sheets.
2 **Adult:** cut out both cardboard pieces and glue them together for additional strength. For hanging, punch a small hole with scissors about 1cm (3/8in) in from outside edge of the cardboard circle.
3 With hole at top, glue pine cones, seed pods and other natural objects onto the cardboard. Use glue generously.
4 **Adult:** tie ribbon into bows, child can then glue them to wreath. Allow wreath to dry overnight. **Adult:** spray wreath with clear gloss enamel.

index

facts & figures

Wherever you live, you'll be able to use our projects with the help of these easy-to-follow conversions. While these conversions are approximate only, the difference between an exact and the approximate conversion of various linear, liquid and dry measures is but minimal and will not affect the results of your projects.

dry measures

metric	imperial
15g	½oz
30g	1oz
60g	2oz
90g	3oz
125g	4oz (¼lb)
155g	5oz
185g	6oz
220g	7oz
250g	8oz (½lb)
280g	9oz
315g	10oz
345g	11oz
375g	12oz (¾lb)
410g	13oz
440g	14oz
470g	15oz
500g	16oz (1lb)
750g	24oz (1½lb)
1kg	32oz (2lb)

liquid measures

metric	imperial
30ml	1 fluid oz
60ml	2 fluid oz
100ml	3 fluid oz
125ml (½ cup)	4 fluid oz
150ml	5 fluid oz (¼ pint/1 gill)
190ml	6 fluid oz
250ml (1 cup)	8 fluid oz
300ml	10 fluid oz (½ pint)
500ml	16 fluid oz
600ml	20 fluid oz (1 pint)
1000ml (1 litre)	1¾ pints

helpful measures

metric	imperial
1cm	⅜in
2cm	¾in
2.5cm	1in
5cm	2in
10cm	4in
15cm	6in
20cm	8in
25cm	10in
30cm	12in (1ft)

Project Editor *Lynne Smith*
Designer *Mary Keep*

Editorial director *Susan Tomnay*
Creative director *Hieu Chi Nguyen*
Publishing manager (sales) *Brian Cearnes*
Publishing manager (rights & new projects)
   Jane Hazell
Brand manager *Donna Gianniotis*
Pre-press *Harry Palmer*
Production manager *Carol Currie*

Publisher *Sue Wannan*
Group publisher *Jill Baker*
Chief executive officer *John Alexander*

Produced by ACP Books, Sydney.

Printing by Tien Wah Press in Singapore.

Published by ACP Publishing Pty Limited,
54 Park St, Sydney; GPO Box 4088, Sydney,
NSW 1028. Ph: (02) 9282 8618
Fax: (02) 9267 9438.
acpbooks@acp.com.au
www.acpbooks.com.au

To order books phone 136 116.

AUSTRALIA Distributed by Network Services,
GPO Box 4088, Sydney, NSW 1028.
Ph: (02) 9282 8777 Fax: (02) 9264 3278.

UNITED KINGDOM Distributed by Australian
Consolidated Press (UK), Moulton Park Business
Centre, Red House Road, Moulton Park,
Northampton, NN3 6AQ. Ph: (01604) 497 531
Fax: (01604) 497 533 acpukltd@aol.com

CANADA Distributed by Whitecap Books Ltd,
351 Lynn Ave, North Vancouver, BC, V7J 2C4,
Ph: (604) 980 9852 Fax: (604) 980 8197
customerservice@whitecap.ca
www.whitecap.ca

NEW ZEALAND Distributed by Netlink Distribution
Company, ACP Media Centre, Cnr Fanshawe and
Beaumont Streets, Westhaven, Auckland.
PO Box 47906, Ponsonby, Auckland, NZ.
Ph: (9) 366 9966 ask@ndcnz.co.nz

Includes index.
For children.
ISBN 1 86396 330 8

1. Handicrafts – Juvenile literature.
2. Creative activities and seat work –
   Juvenile literature.
I. Title: The best of children's art & crafts.
II. Title: Australian women's weekly.

745.5

Cover photography *Getty Images*